TITCOMB'S LETTERS

TO

YOUNG PEOPLE.

SINGLE AND MARRIED.

TIMOTHY TITCOMB, Esquire

TWENTY-FIFTH EDITION.

NEW YORK:
CHARLES SCRIBNER,
No. 124 GRAND STREET.
1861.

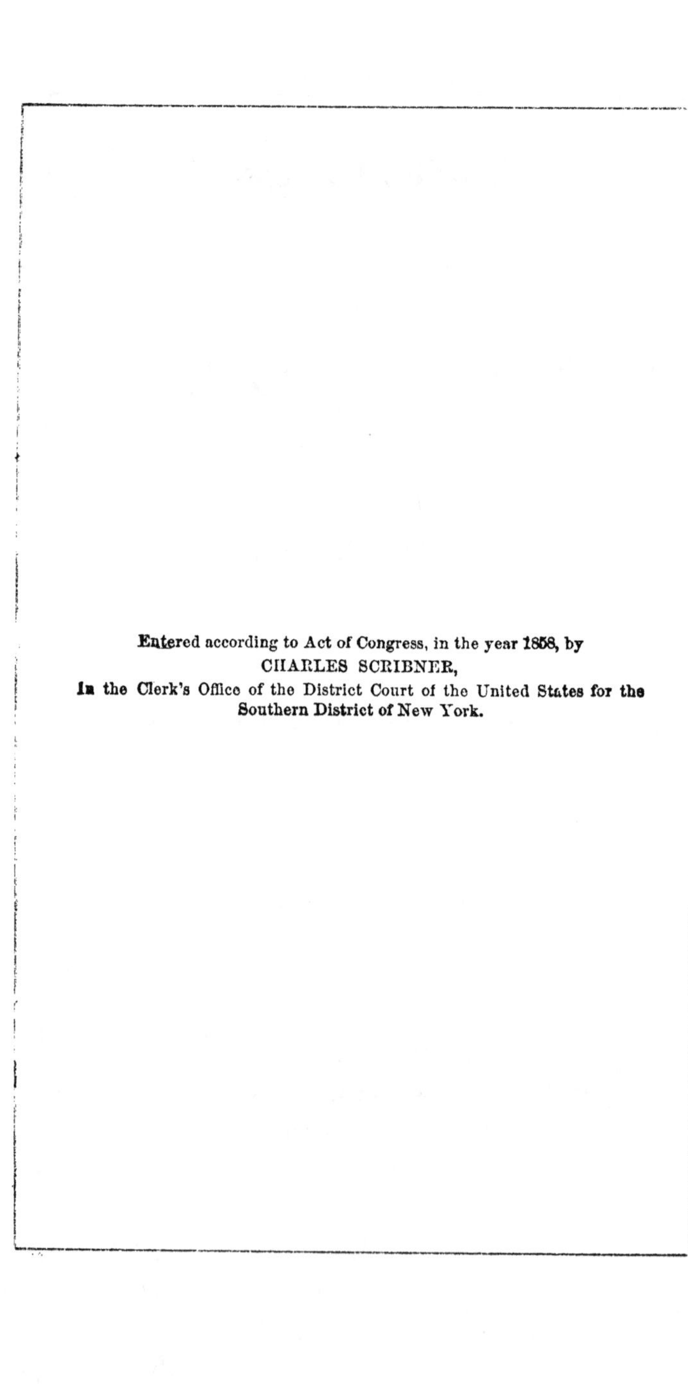

TITCOMB S LETTERS.

TO THE

REV. HENRY WARD BEECHER

You have very kindly permitted me to dedicate this book to you. I do it with hearty pleasure, and with cordial thanks for your courtesy, because it will do me good in several ways. First, it will give me an opportunity to manifest the respect and admiration which I entertain towards one who, in the best way, is doing more than any other American for the elevation of the standard of Christian manhood and womanhood. Second, it will save to me the awkward labor of writing a general preface. One can say to a friend, you know, in a familiar way, what he would hesitate to say directly to the public of his own performances. Third, it will show the public that yo know the author of these letters, and that you have confidence in his good intentions.

The Great Master taught you how to teach, and, if we heed the lesson of His life, He will teach us all. He assumed a sympathetic level with humanity, that He might secure the eye and ear of the world. Through these He obtained the heart—a conquest preliminary to that of the world's understanding and life. It was the divine policy—rather, perhaps, I should say, the eternal necessity—that He should be made in all points like as we are, in order to a fitness for and the fulfilment of his mission. It was the brother that was in Him which touched humanity, and became the medium of heavenly impulses and inspirations; and it is the brother in us, rather than the preceptor, which will enable us to reach the hearts and minds that call for our ministrations.

With this idea in mind, I cannot but think that a general mistake has been made in the instructions given to the young. Most writers have chosen a standpoint distant from, and elevated above, the warm, quick natures which they have addressed. The young have been preached to, lectured to, taught, exhorted, advised, but they have rarely been *talked to.* My aim, in this triple-headed series of letters, is to give brotherly counsel, in a direct and pointed way, to the young men and women of the country, upon subjects which have immediate practical bearing upon their life and destiny, and to give this counsel without a resort to cant, or to the preceptive formularies that so much prevail in didactic literature. I think I know the young, and know what they need; so I have addressed them with this presumption, and with the same freedom—sometimes with the same earnest and emphatic abruptness—that I would use in talking to brothers and sisters whose eyes were looking into mine, whose hands I held.

After all, is there not an assumption of superiority in this? Only that which is necessary for decanting the experiences and the truths which my heart holds into the hearts I seek to fill. A pitcher may have an ear noticeable for length and breadth, and its contents may occupy an inferior level, yet it may brim a goblet with pure water, without other elevation than that which is necessary for the service.

You will notice that I address my letters to the young men, young women, and young married people, as classes, with distinctness of aim and application, while I inclose all in a single volume. I have intended the whole book for each class. I believe that each should know what I have to say to the other. I have written nothing to one class which it would not be well for the other to know. The effort to maintain a divided interest and a divided sympathy between the sexes, to deny to them partnership in a common knowledge of their relationship, to hide them from each other as if they were necessarily enemies or dangerous associates, and to obliterate the idea that they are sharers in the same nature, and companions in a common destiny, may spring from the purest motives, but it produces inhuman results.

I look around me, and I see the young of both sexes with hearts bounding high with hope, forms elastic with health, and eyes bright with the enjoyment of life; and the thought of the stern discipline which awaits them, touches me to tears. Their dawning sun gilds only the mountain-tops of life, and leaves the blind defiles and dismal gorges for their weary feet to find, through years of patient or fretful travel. To tell them how to perform this journey worthily, and to do it hand in hand, in harmonious companionship, I have written these letters. It has been with me an honest and earnest work, in the object of which I am sure that you will sympathize. I only hope that you will find little to criticise and nothing to condemn, in the nature and style of the means by which I have sought to accomplish it.

Yours,

With respectful affection,

THE AUTHOR.

REPUBLICAN OFFICE,
Springfield, July 1, 1858.

CONTENTS.

LETTERS TO YOUNG MEN.

LETTERS TO YOUNG WOMEN.

LETTERS TO YOUNG MARRIED PEOPLE.

LETTERS TO YOUNG MEN.

LETTER I.

GETTING THE RIGHT START.

In idle wishes fools supinely stay,
Be there a will, then wisdom finds a way.

BURNS.

I SUPPOSE that the first great lesson a young man should learn is that he knows nothing; and that the earlier and more thoroughly this lesson is learned, the better it will be for his peace of mind and his success in life. A young man, bred at home, and growing up in the light of parental admiration and fraternal pride, cannot readily understand how it is that every one else can be his equal in talent and acquisition. If, bred in the country, he seeks the life of the town, he will very early obtain an idea of his insignificance. After putting on airs and getting severely laughed at, going into a bright and facile society and finding himself awkward and tongue-tied, undertaking to speak in some public place and breaking down, and paying his addresses to some gentle charmer and receiving for his amiable condescension a mitten of inconvenient dimensions, he will be apt to sit down in a state "bordering on distraction," to reason about it.

This is a critical period in his history. The result of his reasoning will decide his fate. If, at this time, he thoroughly comprehend, and in his soul admit and accept the fact, that he knows nothing and is nothing; if he bow to the conviction that his mind and his person are but ciphers among the significant and cleanly cut figures about him, and that whatever he is to be, and is to win, must be achieved by hard work, there is abundant hope of him. If, on the contrary, a huge self-conceit still hold possession of him, and he straighten stiffly up to the assertion of his old and valueless self; or if he sink discouraged upon the threshold of a life of fierce competitions and more manly emulations, he might as well be a dead man. The world has no use for such a man, and he has only to retire or be trodden upon.

When a young man has thoroughly comprehended the fact that he knows nothing, and that, intrinsically, he is of but little value, the next thing for him to learn is that the world cares nothing for him;—that he is the subject of no man's overwhelming admiration and esteem; that he must take care of himself. A letter of introduction may possibly procure him an invitation to tea. If he wear a good hat, and tie his cravat with propriety, the sexton will show him to a pleasant seat in church, and expect him to contribute liberally when the plate goes round. If he be a stranger, he will find every man busy with his own affairs, and none to look after him. He will not be noticed until he becomes noticeable, and he will not become noticeable until he does something to prove that he has an absolute value in society. No letter of recommendation will give him this, or ought to give him this. No family connexion will give him this, except among those few who think more of blood than brains.

Society demands that a young man shall be somebody, not only, but that he shall prove his right to the title; and it has a right to demand this. Society will not take this matter upon trust—at least, not for a long time, for it has been cheated too frequently. Society is not very particular what a man does, so that it prove him to be a man: then it will bow to him, and make room for him. I know a young man who made a place for himself by writing an article for the North American Review: nobody read the article, so far as I know, but the fact that he wrote such an article, that it was very long, and that it was published, did the business for him. Everybody, however, cannot write articles for the North American Review—at least, I hope everybody will not, for it is a publication which makes me a quarterly visit; but everybody, who is somebody, can do something. There is a wide range of effort between holding a skein of silk for a lady and saving her from drowning—between collecting voters on election day and teaching a Sunday School class. A man must enter society of his own free will, as an active element or a valuable component, before he can receive the recognition that every true man longs for. I take it that this is right. A man who is willing to enter society as a beneficiary is mean, and does not deserve recognition.

There is no surer sign of an unmanly and cowardly spirit than a vague desire for help; a wish to depend, to lean upon somebody, and enjoy the fruits of the industry of others. There are multitudes of young men, I suppose, who indulge in dreams of help from some quarter, coming in at a convenient moment, to enable them to secure the success in life which they covet The vision haunts them of some benevolent old gentleman with a pocket full of money, a trunk full of mortgages and stocks, and a mind remarkably appreciative of merit and genius, who will, perhaps, give or lend them anywhere from ten to twenty thousand dollars, with which they will commence and go on swimmingly.

Perhaps he will take a different turn, and educate them. Or, perhaps, with an eye to the sacred profession, they desire to become the beneficiaries of some benevolent society, or some gentle circle of female devotees.

To me, one of the most disgusting sights in the world is that of a young man with healthy blood, broad shoulders, presentable calves, and a hundred and fifty pounds, more or less, of good bone and muscle, standing with his hands in his pockets, longing for help. I admit that there are positions in which the most independent spirit may accept of assistance—may, in fact, as a choice of evils, desire it; but for a man who is able to help himself, to desire the help of others in the accomplishment of his plans of life, is positive proof that he has received a most unfortunate training, or that there is a leaven of meanness in his composition that should make him shudder. Do not misunderstand me: I would not inculcate that pride of personal independence which repels in its sensitiveness the well-meant good offices nd benefactions of friends, or that resorts to desperate hifts rather than incur an obligation. What I condemn in a young man is the love of dependence; the willingness to be under obligation for that which his own efforts may win.

I have often thought that the Education Society, and kindred organizations, do much more harm than good by inviting into the Christian ministry a class of young men who are willing to be helped. A man who willingly receives assistance, especially if he has applied for it, invariably sells himself to his benefactor, unless that benefactor happen to be a man of sense who is giving absolutely necessary assistance to one whom he knows to be sensitive and honorable. Any young man who will part with freedom and the self-respect that grows out of self-reliance and self-support, is unmanly, neither deserving of assistance, nor capable of making good use of it. Assistance will invariably be received by a young man of spirit as a dire necessity—as the chief evil of his poverty.

When, therefore, a young man has ascertained and fully received the fact that he does not know anything, that the world does not care anything about him, that what he wins must be won by his own brain and brawn, and that while he holds in his own hands the means of gaining his own livelihood and the objects of his life, he cannot receive assistance without compromising his self-respect and selling his freedom, he is in a fair position for beginning life. When a young man becomes aware that only by his own efforts can he rise into companionship and competition with the sharp, strong, and well-drilled minds around him, he is ready for work, and not before.

The next lesson is that of patience, thoroughness of preparation, and contentment with the regular channels of business effort and enterprise. This is, perhaps, one of the most difficult to learn, of all the lessons of life. It is natural for the mind to reach out eagerly for immediate results. As manhood dawns, and the young man catches in its first light the pinnacles of realized dreams, the golden domes of high possibilities, and the purpling hills of great delights, and then looks down upon the narrow, sinuous, long, and dusty path by which others have reached them, he is apt to be disgusted with the passage, and to seek for success through broader channels, by quicker means. Beginning at the very foot of the hill, and working slowly to the top, seems a very discouraging process; and precisely at this point have thousands of young men made shipwreck of their lives.

Let this be understood, then, at starting; that the patient conquest of difficulties which rise in the regular and legitimate channels of business and enterprise, is not cnly essential in securing the successes which you seek, but it is essential to that preparation of your mind requisite for the enjoyment of your successes, and for retaining them when gained. It is the general rule of Providence, the world over, and in all time, that unearned success is a curse. It is the rule of Providence, that the process of earning success shall be the preparation for its conservation and enjoyment. So, day by day, and week by week; so, month after month, and year after year, work on, and in that process gain strength and symmetry, and nerve and knowledge, that when success, patiently and bravely worked for, shall come, it may find you prepared to receive it and keep it. The development which you will get in this brave and patient labor, will prove itself, in the end, the most valuable of your successes. It will help to make a man of you. It will give you power and self-reliance. It will give you not only self-respect, but the respect of your fellows and the public.

Never allow yourself to be seduced from this course. You will hear of young men who have made fortunes in some wild speculations. Pity them; for they will almost certainly lose their easily won success. Do not be in a hurry for anything. Are you in love with some dear girl, whom you would make your wife? Give Angelina Matilda to understand that she must wait; and if Angelina Matilda is really the good girl you take er to be, she will be sensible enough to tell you to choose your time. You cannot build well without first laying a good foundation; and for you to enter upon a business which you have not patiently and thoroughly learned, and to marry before you have won a character, or even the reasonable prospect of a competence, is ultimately to bring your house down about the ears of

Angelina Matilda, and such pretty children as she may give you. If, at the age of thirty years, you find yourself established in a business which pays you with certainty a living income, you are to remember that God has blessed you beyond the majority of men.

In saying what I have said to you in this letter, I have had no wish to make of you pattern young men; but of this I will speak more fully hereafter. The fashion plates of the magazines bear no striking resemblance to the humanity which we meet in the streets. I only seek to give you the principles and the spirit which should animate you, without any attempt or desire to set before you the outlines of the life I would have you lead. In fact, if there are detestable things which I despise above all other things detestable, they are the patterns made for young men, and the young men made after them. I would have you carry all your individuality with you, all your blood well purified, all your passions well controlled and made tributary to the motive forces of your nature; all your manhood. enlarged, ennobled, and uncorrupted; all your piety, rendering your whole being sensitively alive to your relations to God and man; all your honor, your affections, and your faculties—all these, and still hold yourselves strictly amenable to those laws which confine a true success to the strong and constant hand of patient achievement.

LETTER II.

FEMALE SOCIETY—THE WOMAN FOR A WIFE.

O woman! lovely woman! Nature made thee
To temper man; we had been brutes without you.
Angels are painted fair to look like you.

OTWAY.

When I said I would die a bachelor, I did not think that I should live till I were married.

SHAKSPERE.

IN many of the books addressed to young men, a great deal is said about the purifying and elevating influences of female society. Sentimental young men affect this kind of reading, and if anywhere in it they can find countenance for the policy of early marriage, they are delighted. Now, while I will be the last to deny the purifying and elevating influence of pure and elevated women, I do deny that there is anything in indiscriminate devotion to female society, which makes a man better or purer. Suppose a man cast away on the Cannibal Islands, and not in sufficiently good flesh to excite the appetites of the gentle epicureans among whom he has fallen. Suppose him, in fact, to be "received into society," and made the private secretary of a king without a liberal education. Suppose, after awhile, he feels himself subsiding into a state of barbarism, and casts around for some redeeming or conservative influence. At this moment it occurs to him that in the trunk on which he sailed ashore were a number of books. He flies to the trunk, and, in an ecstasy of delight, discovers that among them is a volume addressed to young men. He opens it eagerly, and finds the writer to declare that next to the Christian religion, there is nothing that will tend so strongly to the elevation and purification of young men, as female society. He accordingly seeks the society of women, and drinks in the marvellous influences of their presence. He finds them unacquainted with some of the most grateful uses of water, and in evident ignorance of the existence of ivory combs. About what year of the popular era is it to be supposed that he will arrive at a desirable state of purification and perfection?

Now, perhaps you do not perceive the force of this illustration. Let us get at it, then. When you find yourself shut out from all female society except that which is beneath you, that society will do you just as much and no more good than that of the fair cannibals, especially if it be young. If, in all this society, you can find one old woman of sixty, who has common sense genial good-nature, experience, some reading, and sympathetic heart, cherish her as you would her weight in gold, but let the young trash go. You will hear nothing from them but gossip and nonsense, and you will only get disgusted with the world and yourself. Inspiration to higher and purer life always comes from above a man; and female society can only elevate and purify a man when it is higher and purer than he is. In the element of purity, I doubt not that women generally are superior to men, but it is very largely a negative or unconscious element, and has not the power and influence of a positive virtue.

Therefore, whenever you seek for female society, as an agency in the elevation of your tastes, the preservation of your morals, and the improvement of your mind, seek for that which is above you. I do not counsel you to treat with rudeness or studied neglect such inferio female society as you are obliged to come in contact with. On the contrary, you owe such society a duty. You should stimulate it, infuse new life into it, if possible, and do for it what you would have female society do for yourself.

This matter of seeking female society above yourself you should carry still further. Never content yourself with the idea of having a common-place wife. You want one who will stimulate you, stir you up, keep you moving, show you your weak points, and make something of you. Don't fear that you cannot get such a wife. I very well remember the reply which a gentleman who happened to combine the qualities of wit and common sense, made to a young man who expressed a fear that a certain young lady of great beauty and attainments would dismiss him, if he should become serious. "My friend," said the wit, "infinitely more beautiful and accomplished women than she is, have married infinitely uglier and meaner men than you are." And such is the fact. If you are honest and honorable, if your character is spotless, if you are enterprising and industrious, if you have some grace and a fair degree of sense, and if you love appreciatingly and truly, you can marry almost anybody worth your having. So, to encourage yourself, carry in your memory the above aphorism reduced to a form something like this: "Infinitely finer women than I ever expect to marry, have loved and married men infinitely meaner than I am."

The apprehensions of women are finer and quicker than those of men. With equal early advantages, the woman is more of a woman at eighteen than a man is a man at twenty-one. After marriage, as a genera thing, the woman ceases to acquire. Now, I do not say that this is necessary, or that it should be the case, but I simply state a general fact. The woman is absorbed in family cares, or perhaps devotes from ten to twenty years to the bearing and rearing of children—the most dignified, delightful, and honorable office of her life. This consumes her time, and, in a great multitude of instances, deprives her of intellectual culture.

In the meantime, the man is out, engaged in business. He comes in daily contact with minds stronger and sharper than his own. He grows and matures, and in ten years from the date of his marriage, becomes, in reality, a new man. Now, if he was so foolish as to marry a woman because she had a pretty form and face, or sweet eyes, or an amiable disposition, or a pleasant temper, or wealth, he will find that he has passed entirely by his wife, and that she is really no more of a companion for him than a child would be. I know of but few sadder sights in this world than that of mates whom the passage of years has mis-mated. A woman ought to have a long start of a man, and then, ten to one, the man will come out ahead in the race of a long life.

I suppose that in every young man's mind there exist the hope and the expectation of marriage. When a young man pretends to me that he has no wish to marry, and that he never expects to marry, I always infer one of two things: that he lies, and is really very anxious for marriage, or that his heart has been polluted by association with unworthy women. In a thousand cases we shall not find three exceptions to this rule. A young man who, with any degree of earnestness, declares that he intends never to marry, confesses to a brutal nature or perverted morals.

But how shall a good wife be won? I know that men naturally shrink from the attempt to obtain companions who are their superiors; but they will find that really intelligent women, who possess the most desirable qualities, are uniformly modest, and hold their charms in modest estimation. What such women most admire in men is gallantry; not the gallantry of courts and fops, but boldness, courage, devotion, decision, and refined civility. A man's bearing wins ten superior women where his boots and brains win one. If a man stand before a woman with respect for himself and fearessness of her, his suit is half won. The rest may safely be left to the parties most interested. Therefore, never be afraid of a woman. Women are the most harmless and agreeable creatures in the world, to a man who shows that he has got a man's soul in him. If you have not got the spirit in you to come up to a test like this, you have not got that in you which most pleases a high-souled woman, and you will be obliged to content yourself with the simple girl who, in a quiet way, is endeavoring to attract and fasten you.

But don't be in a hurry about the matter. Don't go into a feverish longing for marriage. It isn't creditable to you. Especially don't imagine that any disappointment in love which takes place before you are twenty-one years old will be of any material damage to you. The truth is, that before a man is twenty-five years old he does not know what he wants himself. So don't be in a hurry. The more of a man you become, and the more of manliness you become capable of exhibiting in your association with women, the better wife you will be able to obtain; and one year's possession of the heart and hand of a really noble specimen of her sex, is worth nine hundred and ninety-nine years' possession of a sweet creature with two ideas in her head, and nothing new to say about either of them. "Better fifty years of Europe than a cycle of Cathay." So don't be in a hurry, I say again. You don't want a wife now and you have not the slightest idea of the kind of wife you will want by-and-by. Go into female society if you can find that which will improve you, but not otherwise. You can spend your time better. Seek the society of good men. That is often more accessible to you than the other, and it is through that mostly that you will find your way to good female society.

If any are disposed to complain of the injustice to woman of advice like this, and believe that it involves a wrong to her, I reply that not the slightest wrong is intended. Thorough appreciation of a good woman, on the part of a young man, is one of his strongest recommendations to her favor. The desire of such a man to possess and associate his life with such a woman, gives evidence of qualities, aptitudes, and capacities which entitle him to any woman's consideration and respect. There is something good in him; and however uncultivated he may be—however rude in manner, and rough in person—he only needs development to become worthy of her, in some respects, at least. I shall not quarrel with a woman who desires a husband superior to herself, for I know it will be well for her to obtain such an one, if she will be stimulated by contact with a higher mind to a brighter and broader development. At the same time, I must believe that for a man to marry his inferior, is to call upon himself a great misfortune; to deprive himself of one of the most elevating and refining influences which can possibly affect him. I therefore believe it to be the true policy of every young man to aim high in his choice of a companion. I have previously given a reason for this policy, and both that and this conspire to establish the soundness of my counsel.

One thing more: not the least important, but the last in this letter. No woman without piety in he heart is fit to be the companion of any man. You may get, in your wife, beauty, amiability, sprightliness, wit, accomplishments, wealth, and learning, but if that wife have no higher love than herself and yourself, she is a poor creature. She cannot elevate you above mean aims and objects, she cannot educate her children properly, she cannot in hours of adversity sustain and comfort you, she cannot bear with patience your petulance induced by the toils and vexations of business, and she will never be safe against the seductive temptations of gaiety and dress.

Then, again, a man who has the prayers of a pious wife, and knows that he has them—upheld by heaven, or by a refined sense of obligation and gratitude—can rarely become a very bad man. A daily prayer from the heart of a pure and pious wife, for a husband engrossed in the pursuits of wealth or fame, is a chain of golden words that links his name every day with the name of God. He may snap it three hundred and sixty-five times in a year, for many years, but the chances are that in time he will gather the sundered filaments, and seek to re-unite them in an everlasting bond.

LETTER III.

MANNERS AND DRESS.

So over violent, or over civil,
That every man with him was God or devil.

DRYDEN

Costly thy habit as thy purse can buy,
But not expressed in fancy; rich, not gaudy;
For the apparel oft proclaims the man.

SHAKSPERE.

IT is well for young men to obtain, at the very start of their career, some idea of the value of politeness. Some cannot be otherwise than urbane. They are born so. One can kick them roundly and soundly, and they will not refuse to smile, if it be done good-naturedly. They dodge all corners by a necessity of their nature. If their souls had only corporeal volume, we could see them making their way through a crowd, like nice little spaniels, scaring nobody, running between nobody's legs, but winding along shrinkingly and gracefully, seeing a master in every man, and thus flattering every man's vanity into good-nature, but really spoiling their reputation as reliable dogs, by their undiscriminating and universal complaisance. There is a self-forgetfulness which is so deep as to be below self-respect, and such instances as we occasionally meet with should be treated compassionately, like cases of idiocy or insanity, except when found in connexion with the post-office department or among hotel waiters.

But puppyism is not really politeness. The genuine article is as necessary to success, and particularly to an enjoyable success, as integrity, or industry, or any other indispensable thing. All machinery ruins itself by friction, without the presence of a lubricating fluid. Politeness, or civility, or urbanity, or whatever we may choose to call it, is the oil which preserves the machinery of society from destruction. We are obliged to bend to one another—to step aside and let another pass, to ignore this and that personal peculiarity, to speak pleasantly when irritated, and to do a great many things to avoid abrasion and collision. In other words, in a world of selfish interests and pursuits, where every man is pursuing his own special good, we must mask our real designs in studied politeness, or mingle them with real kindness, in order to elevate the society of men above the society of wolves. Young men generally would doubtless be thoroughly astonished if they could comprehend at a single glance how greatly their personal happiness, popularity, prosperity, and usefulness depend on their manners.

I know young men who, in the discharge of their duties, imagine that if they go through them with a literal performance, they are doing all that they undertake to do. You will never see a smile upon their faces, nor hear a genial word of good fellowship from their lips; and from the manner in which their labor is performed you would never learn that they were engaged in intercourse with human beings. They carry the same manner and the same spirit into the counting-room that they do into the dog-kennel or the stable. Everybody hates such young men as these, and recoils from all contact with them. If they have business with them, they close it as soon as possible, and get out of their presence. A man who, having got his vessel under headway on the voyage of life, takes a straight course, minding nothing for the man-of-war that lies in his path, or the sloop that crosses his bow, or the fishing smacks that find game where he seeks nothing but a passage, or interposing rocks or islands, will be very sure to get terribly rubbed before he gets through—and he ought to be.

I despise servility, but true and uniform politeness is the glory of any young man. It should be a politeness full of frankness and good-nature, unobtrusive and constant, and uniform in its exhibition to every class of men. The young man who is overwhelmingly polite to a celebrity or a nabob, and rude to a poor Irishman because he is a poor Irishman, deserves to be despised. That style of manners which combines self-respect with respect for the rights and feelings of others, especially if it be warmed up by the fires of a genial heart, is a thing to be coveted and cultivated, and it is a thing that pays, alike in cash and comfort.

The talk of manners introduces us naturally to dress and personal appearance. I believe in dress. I believe that it is the duty of all men—young and old—to make their persons, so far as practicable or possible, agreeable to those with whom they are thrown into association. I mean by this that they shall not offend by singularity, nor by slovenliness; that they shall "make a conscience" of clean boots and finger-nails, change their linen twice a week, and not show themselves in shirt-sleeves if they can help it. Let no man know by your dress what your business is. You dress your person, not your trade. You are, if you know enough, to mould the fashion of the time to your own personal peculiarities—to make it your servant, and not allow it to be your master. Never dress in extremes. Let there always be a hint in your dress that you know the style, but, for the best of reasons, disregard its more extreme demands. The best possible impression that you can make by your dress is to make no separate impression at all; but so to harmonize its material and shape with your personality, that it becomes tributary in the general effect, and so exclusively tributary that people cannot tell after seeing you what kind of clothes you wear. They will only remember that you look well, and somehow dress becomingly.

I suppose that I shall be met here with a protest from employers, and a kind of protest from the employed. Counsel to dress well is dangerous, is it? But everybody now dresses extravagantly; and, as extravagant dressing is usually very far from good dressing, I think that the danger of exciting greater extravagance is very small. It may be descending into pretty small particulars, but it is proper to say that some men can dress better on fifty dollars a year than others can on one hundred, and for reasons which it is my duty to disclose. There was something in the doctrine of the loafer who maintained that "extremes justify the means," illustrating his proposition by wearing faultless hat and boots and leaving the rest of his person in rags; but he had not touched the real philosophy of the matter.

There is on every man what may be called a *dress-centre*—a nucleus from which the rest of the dress should be developed, and unfolded. This dress-centre, or primary dress idea, is different in different persons, but it is always above the waist. The cravat, the vest, the hat, the bosom, the coat-collar, may either of them be this idea. It is always safe to locate it about the neck and chest. A beautiful cravat, sustaining a faultless dicky, is about all a man can stand without damage, in the way of elegant dress. This should form the centre. The vest should harmonize, but be modest, and all the other robing should be shaded off, until there is not an obtrusive feature. Extremities will then only be noticed. These should be faultlessly dressed, but in a manner rather to satisfy than attract attention. Everything should be subordinated to this idea; the whole dress should bow to the cravat. Any man who has made dress a study knows very well that ten dollars a year, spent about the neck, will go further than fifty dollars spread upon the person. Coarsest clothes, developed from an elegant neck-tie, or an elegant central idea of any kind, become elegant themselves, and receive and evolve a glory which costs absolutely nothing at all, except a few brains, some consideration, and the reading of this letter.

One sees the demonstration of this in travelling. We

meet multitudes from all quarters and of different nationalities. One, and he is usually a Yankee, wears the best of broadcloth, and the costliest of coats, and looks vulgar; while another with a single stamp of good taste upon him, at some central point, is a gentleman at half price. Rich clothes are really a sign of mental poverty. Let the secret of good dressing be thoroughly learned, and we shall hear comparatively little of the cost of dress. Let each young man choose his central idea, plant it and develop it; and if he has good common sense he will find that he can dress better than he ever could before, with the expenditure of half the money it has usually cost him.

LETTER IV

BAD HABITS.

There's nothing ill can dwell in such a temple:
If the ill spirit have so fair a house
Good things will strive to dwell with't.

SHAKSPERE.

He that has light within his own clear breast
May sit i' the centre and enjoy bright day;
But he that hides a dark soul and foul thoughts,
Benighted walks under the mid-day sun.

MILTON.

IT is entirely natural for people to form habits, so tha if bad habits be avoided, the good ones will gene rally take care of themselves. I had no intention when I commenced these letters of saying anything upon dogmatic theology, but I take the liberty of suggesting to those who are interested in this kind of thing that if there be anything that demonstrates total depravity, it is the readiness with which young men imbibe bad habits. I have seen original sin in the shape of "a short six" sticking out of the mouth of a lad of ten years. It is strange what particular pains boys and young men will take to learn to do that which will make them miserable, ruin their health, render them disgusting to their friends, and damage their reputation.

Some of the fashionable bad habits of the day are connected with the use of tobacco. Here is a drug that a young man is obliged to become accustomed to before he can tolerate either the taste or the effect of it. It is a rank vegetable poison; and in the unaccustomed animal produces vertigo, faintness, and horrible sickness. Yet young men persevere in the use of it until they can endure it, and then until they love it. They go about the streets with cigars in their mouths, or into society with breath sufficiently offensive to drive all unperverted nostrils before them. They chew tobacco—roll up huge wads of the vile drug and stuff their cheeks with them. They ejaculate their saliva upon the sidewalk, in the store, in spittoons which become incorporate stenches, in dark corners of railroad cars to stain the white skirts of unsuspecting women, in lecture-rooms and churches, upon fences, and into stoves that hiss with anger at the insult. And the quids after they are ejected! They are to be found in odd corners, in out-of-the-way places—great boul ders, boluses, bulbs! Horses stumble over them, dogs bark at them; they poison young shade-trees, and break down the constitutions of sweepers. This may be an exaggeration of the facts, but not of the disgust with which one writes of them.

Now, young men, just think of this thing! You are born into the world with a sweet breath. At a proper age, you acquire a good set of teeth. Why will you make of one a putrescent exhalation, and of the other a set of yellow pegs? A proper description of the habit of chewing tobacco would exhaust the filthy adjectives of the language, and spoil the adjectives themselves for further use; and yet, you will acquire the habit, and persist in it after it is acquired! It is very singular that young men will adopt a habit of which every man who is its victim is ashamed. There is, probably, no tobacco-chewer in the world who would advise a young man to commence this habit. I have never seen a slave of tobacco who did not regret his bondage; yet, against all advice, against nausea and disgust, against cleanliness, against every consideration of health and comfort, thousands every year bow the neck to this drug, and consent to wear its repulsive yoke. They will chew it; they will smoke it in cigars and pipes until their bed-rooms and shops cannot be breathed in, and until their breath is as rank as the breath of a foul beast, and their clothes have the odor of the sewer. Some of them take snuff; cram the fiery weed up their nostrils to irritate that subtle sense which rarest flowers were made to feed--in all this working against God, abusing nature, perverting sense, injuring health, planting the seeds of disease, and insulting the decencies of life and the noses of the world.

So much for the nature of the habit; and I would stop here, but for the fact that I am in earnest, and wish to present every motive in my power to prevent young men from forming the habit, or persuade them to abandon it. The habit of using tobacco is expensive. A clerk on a modest salary has no right to be seen with a cigar in his mouth. Three cigars a day, at five cents apiece, amount to more than fifty dollars a year. Can you afford it? You know you cannot. You know that to do this you have either got to run in debt or steal. Therefore I say that you have no business to be seen with a cigar in your mouth. It is presumptive vidence against your moral character.

Did it ever occur to you what you are, what you are made for, whither you are going? That beautiful body of yours, in whose construction infinite wisdom exhausted the resources of its ingenuity, is the temple of a soul that shall live for ever, a companion of angels, a searcher into the deep things of God, a being allied in essence to the divine. I say the body is the temple, or the tabernacle, of such a being as this; and what do you hink of stuffing the front door of such a building full of the most disgusting weeds that you can find, or setting a slow match to it, or filling the chimneys with snuff? It looks to me much like an endeavor to smoke out the tenant, or to insult him in such a manner as to induce him to quit the premises. You really ought to be ashamed of such behavior. A clean mouth, a sweet breath, unstained teeth, and inoffensive clothing—are not these treasures worth preserving? Then throw away tobacco, and all thoughts of it, at once and for ever. Be a man. Be decent, and be thankful to me for talking so plainly to you.

But there are other bad habits besides the use of tobacco. There is the habit of using strong drink,—not the habit of getting drunk, with most young men, but the habit of taking drink occasionally in its milder forms—of playing with a small appetite that only needs sufficient playing with to make you a demon or a dolt You think you are safe. I know you are not safe, if you drink at all; and when you get offended with the good friends who warn you of your danger, I know you are a fool. I know that the grave swallows daily, by scores, drunkards, every one of whom thought he was safe while he was forming his appetite. But this is old talk. A young man in this age who forms the habit of drinking, or puts himself in danger of forming the habit, is usually so weak that it doesn't pay to save him.

I pass by profanity. That is too offensive and vulgar a habit for any man who reads a respectable book to indulge in. I pass by this, I say; to come to a habit more destructive than any I have contemplated.

Young man! you who are so modest in the presence of women,—so polite and amiable; you who are invited into families where there are pure and virtuous girls; you who go to church, and seem to be such a pattern young man; you who very possibly neither smoke, nor chew, nor snuff, nor swear, nor drink—you have one habit ten times worse than all these put together,—a habit that makes you a whited sepulchre, fair without, but within full of dead men's bones and all uncleanness. You have a habit of impure thought, that poisons the very springs of your life. It may lead you into lawless indulgences, or it may not. So far as your character is concerned, it makes little difference. A young man wh cherishes impure images, and indulges in impure conversations with his associates, is poisoned. There is rottenness in him. He is not to be trusted. Hundreds of thousands of men are living in unhappiness and degradation to-day who owe their unhappy lives to an early habit of impure thought. To a young man who has become poisoned in this way, women all appear to be vicious or weak; and when a young man loses his respect for the sex made sacred by the relations of mother and sister, he stands upon the crumbling edge of ruin. His sensibilities are killed, and his moral nature almost beyond the reach of regeneration. I believe it to be true that a man who has lost his belief in woman has, as a general thing, lost his faith in God.

The only proper way to treat such a habit as this is to fly from it—discard it—expel it—fight it to the death. Impure thought is a moral drug quite as seductive and poisonous to the soul as tobacco is to the body. It perverts the tone of every fibre of the soul. One should have more respect for his body than to make it the abode of toads and lizards and unclean reptiles of all sorts. The whole matter resolves itself into this: A young man is not fit for life until he is clean—clean and healthy, body and soul, with no tobacco in his mouth, no liquor in his stomach, no oath on his tongue, no snuff in is nose, and no thought in his heart which if exposed would send him sneaking into darkness from the presence of good women. I know a man who believes that the regeneration of the world is to be brought about by a change of diet. If he will add the policy of utter cleaniness to his scheme, I will agree not to quarrel with him.

LETTER V.

THE BLESSINGS OF POVERTY—OFFICE AND EFFECT OF A PROFESSION.

> The labor we delight in physics pain.
>
> SHAKSPERE.

> Worth makes the man, and want of it the fellow;
> The rest is all but leather and prunello.
>
> POPE.

IF there is anything in the world that a young man should be more grateful for than another, it is the poverty which necessitates starting life under very great disadvantages. Poverty is one of the best tests of human quality in existence. A triumph over it is like graduating with honor from West Point. It demonstrates stuff and stamina. It is a certificate of worthy labor, faithfully performed. A young man who cannot stand this test is not good for anything. He can never rise above a drudge or a pauper. A young man who cannot feel his will harden as the yoke of poverty presses upon him, and his pluck rise with every difficulty that poverty throws in his way, may as well retire into ome corner, and hide himself. Poverty saves a thousand times more men than it ruins, for it only ruins those who are not particularly worth saving, while it saves multitudes of those whom wealth would have ruined. If any young man who reads this letter is so unfortunate as to be rich, I give him my pity. I pity you, my rich young friend, because you are in danger. You lack one great stimulus to effort and excellence which your poor companion possesses. You will be very apt, if you have a soft spot in your head, to think yourself above him, and that sort of thing makes you mean, and injures you. With full pockets and full stomach, and good linen and broadcloth on your back, your heart and soul will get plethoric, and in the race of life you will find yourself surpassed by all the poor boys around you, before you know it.

No, my boy, if you are poor, thank God and take courage; for he intends to give you a chance to make something of yourself. If you had plenty of money, ten chances to one it would spoil you for all useful purposes. Do you lack education? Have you been cut short in the text books? Remember that education, like some other things, does not consist in the multitude of things a man possesses. What can you *do?* That is the question that settles the business for you. Do you know your business? Do you know men, and how to deal with them? Has your mind, by any means whatsoever, received that discipline which gives to its action power and facility? If so, then you are more of a man, and a thousand times better educated, than the fellow who graduates from a college with his brains full of stuff that he cannot apply to the practical business of life—stuff the acquisition of which has been in no sense a disciplinary process, so far as he is concerned. There are very few men in this world less than thirty years of age, and unmarried, who can afford to be rich. One of the greatest benefits to be reaped from great financial disasters, is the saving of a large crop of young men.

In regard to the choice of a profession, that is your business, and not mine, nor that of any of your friends. If you take to a trade or profession, don't be persuaded out of it, until you are perfectly satisfied that you are not adapted to it. You will receive all sorts of the most excellent advice, but you must remember that if you follow it, and it leads you into a profession that starves you, those who gave the advice never feel bound to give you any money. You have got to take care of yourself in this world, and you may as well choose your own way of doing it, always remembering that it is not your trade nor your profession which makes you respectable. This leads me to a matter that I may as well dispose of here as anywhere.

I propose to explain what I meant in a previous letter by the counsel to "let no man know by your dress what your business is. You dress your person, not your trade." As the proper explanation of this involves a very important principle, I will devote the rest of this letter to its development and illustration. The fault found with this counsel is that it has always been considered best to dress according to one's business and position.

Manhood, and profession or handicraft, are entirely different things; and I wish particularly that every young man engaged in reading these letters should understand the reason why. God makes men, and men make blacksmiths, tailors, farmers, horse jockeys, tradesmen of all sorts, governors, judges, &c. The offices of men may be more or less important, and of higher or lower quality, but manhood is a higher possession than office. An occupation is never an end of life. It is an instrument put into our hands, or taken into our hands, by which to gain for the body the means of living until sickness or old age robs it of life, and we pass on to the world for which this is a preparation. However thoroughly acquired and assiduously followed, a trade is something to be held at arm's length. I can illustrate what I mean by placing, side by side, two horses,—one, fresh from the stall, with every hair in its right place his head up and mane flying, and another that has been worked in the same harness every day for three years, until the skin is bare on each hip and thigh, an inflamed abrasion glows on each side of the back-bone where the hard saddle-pad rests, a severe gall-mark spreads its brown patch under the breast collar, and all the other marks of an abused horse abound. Now a trade, or a profession, will wear into a man as a harness wears into a horse. One can see the "trade mark" on almost every soul and body met in the street. A trade has taken some men by the shoulders and shaken their humanity out of them. It has so warped the natures of others that they might be wet down and set in the sun to dry a thousand times without being warped back.

Thus, I say, a man's trade or profession should be kept at arm's length. It should not be allowed to tyrannize over him, to mould him, to crush him. It should not occupy the whole of his attention. So far from this, it should be regarded, in its material aspect, at least, only as a means for the development of manhood. The great object of living is the attainment of true manhood—the cultivation of every power of the soul and of every high spiritual quality, naturally inherent or graciously superadded. The trade is beneath the man, and should be kept there. With this idea in your minds—and you may be very sure that it is the correct idea—just look around you, and see how almost everybody has missed it. You and I both know physicians whose mental possessions, beyond their knowledge of drugs and diseases, are not worth anything. We are acquainted with lawyers who are never seen out of their offices, who live among pigeon-holes and red tape, and busy their minds with quirks and quarrels so unremittingly, that they have not a thought for other subjects. They are not men at all; they are nothing but lawyers. Often we find not more than five whole men in a town of five thousand inhabitants. Those who pass for men, and who really do get married and have families, are a hundred to one fractional men, or exclusively machines.

Elihu Burritt cultivated the man that was in him until his trade and his blacksmith's shop would not stay with him. They ceased to be useful to him. He could get a living in a way that was better for him. Benjamin Franklin was an excellent printer, but he used his trade only as a means. The development of his mind and his manhood went on above it. Printing with him was not an end of life. If it had been, we should have missed his words of wisdom; some one else would have built the kite that exchanged the first kiss with electricity, and less able men would have been set to do the work which he did so creditably in the management of his country's affairs. It is not necessary that you be learned blacksmiths or philosophical and diplomatic printers, but it is necessary that you be a man before your calling, behind your calling, above your calling, outside of your calling, and inside of it; and that that calling modify your character no more than it would were it your neighbor's.

If I have made my point plain to you, you can readily see that I attach very little value to the distinctions in society based on callings, and still less to those based on office. If a man be a man, let him thank his stars that he is not a justice of the peace. Of all the appetites that curse young men, the appetite for office seems to me to be the silliest and the meanest. There is nothing which fills me with greater disgust than to see a young man eager for the poor distinction which office confers. An office seeker, for the sake of honor, is constitutionally, necessarily, mean. I have seen men begin at twenty-one as prudential committees in small school districts, and stick to office until everybody was sick of them. Whether it rained porridge or potatoes, paving stones or pearls, their dish was always out. They and their families always had to be cared for.

Office always brings obligation and a certain kind of slavery. It brings something more than this—it brings insanity. A young man who allows himself to get a taste of it very rarely recovers. It is like tobacco, o opium, or brandy, producing a morbid appetite; anc we need all through the nation, a new society of re form. There should be a pledge circulated, and everywhere signed, promising total abstinence from office-seeking. To this every young man should put his name. There are chronic cases that may be considered hopeless, but the young can be saved.

Do not let me be misunderstood; I have spoken of the thirst for office for the sake of office. My belief is that office should neither be sought for nor lightly refused. The curse of our country is that office-seekers have made place so contemptible that good men will not accept it, but so far keep themselves removed from politics that all the affairs of government fall into unworthy hands. When a young man is sought for tc fill a responsible place in public affairs—sought for and elected on the ground of fitness—he should decid whether he owes that duty to the public, and perform it well if he does. Office was properly regarded in the "good old colony times." Then it was considered a hindrance to business, and almost or quite a hardship; so much so that laws were passed, in some instances, compelling men to accept office, or pay a fine. So I would have you to do your duty to the public at all times, and especially in seeing that office-seekers, by profession or constant practice, are crowded from the track, and worthy men put on.

LETTER VI.

FOOD AND PHYSICAL CULTURE.

Man is the noblest growth our realms supply,
And souls are ripened in our northern sky.

MRS. BARBAULD.

I HAVE noticed that most writers of books for young men have a good deal to say about diet and regimen, and physical culture, and all that sort of thing, those knowing the least of these important subjects invariably being the most elaborate and specific in their treatment of them. There have been some awful sins committed in this business. All the spare curses I accumulate I dedicate to those white-livered, hatchet-faced, thin-blooded, scrawny reformers, who prescribe sawdust puddings and plank beds, and brief sleep, and early walks, and short commons for the rising generation. I despise them; and if there is a being who always touches the profoundest depths of my sympathy, it is a young man who has become a victim to their notions. It is a hard sight to see a young man with the pluck all taken out of him by a meagre diet—his whole natur starved, degenerated, emasculated.

I propose to apply a little common sense to this business. If I have a likely Durham steer, which I wish to have grow into the full development of his breed, I keep him on something more than a limited quantity of bog hay. I do not stir him up with a pitchfork before he has his nap out, and insist on his being driven ten miles before he has anything to eat. I do not take pains to give him the meanest bed I can find for him. I know perfectly well that that animal will not grow up strong and sound, fat and full, the pride of the farm and the gem of the stall, unless I give him an abundance of the best food, a clean and comfortable place to sleep in, and just as long naps as he sees fit to take. The horse, which in its organization more nearly approaches man than the steer, is still more sensitive to the influence of generous living. How much pluck and spirit will a horse get out of a ton of rye straw? The truth is, that a good and abundant diet is not only essential to the highest physical health and development of man, but it modifies very importantly the development and manifestation of the soul. A man cannot acquire courage by feeding on theories and milk. An Englishman cannot fight without beef in his belly; and no more can any of us.

It may be objected to this that we do not wish for a great animal development in man. I say we do. I declare that the more perfect a man can make his animal nature the better. That animal nature is the associate—home—servant—of the soul. If it be not well developed, in all its organs and in all its functions, it will neither give a generous entertainment to the spiritual thing that dwells in it, nor serve it with vigor and efficiency. If strong meat nurses your passions, let it; it does not nurse your passions any more than it nurses all the rest of you, and if you grow symmetrically where is the harm? Besides, what would you be without passions? They are the impelling forces of life. A man with no passion is as useless in the world as if he were without brains. He cannot even acquire the possession of virtue, but is obliged to content himself with innocence. If God gave passions to a man, he gave them to him for a natural, full development; and the grandest type of man we see is that in which we find fully developed and thoroughly trained passions; and a soul which has not these among its motive forces is like a sailor out at sea, in a skiff without oars. This idea that the body is something to be contemned, that its growth and development must necessarily antagonize with the best growth and development of the soul, is essentially impious. No matter where it started—it is all wrong. A perverted and perverting passion is a fearful thing, but a passion in its place is like everything that God makes, "very good."

I would have you properly understand this kind of talk. I counsel the use of no food that tends to the stimulation of one portion of your system more than another, but I ask you to remember that the best food is not too good for you, and that, unless you have a perverted appetite, there is very little danger of your eating too much of it. If I were to be charged with the special mission of degrading a nation, in mind and body—stunting the form, and weakening in the same proportion the mental and moral nature—there is no way in which I could so readily accomplish my object as through food. No nation can preserve its vitality, and its tendency to progress, with a diet of pork and potatoes. Nothing but the *cerealia* and the *ruminantia* will do for this—nothing but bread and muscle.

I wish I could take you to one of those institutions which will be found in nearly every State, where the outcast and pauper children are gathered for shelter, care, and culture. They come from the gutters, where they have lived on garbage and cold potatoes. Their eyes are red around the edges and very weak, their muscles are flabby, their skin is lifeless in color and in fact. Their minds are as dull as the minds of brutes, and their faces give the impression almost of idiotic stupidity. In six months, wheat and corn bread give them a new body, and a new soul; and it would be difficult to find a brighter set of faces than fill those crowded halls and illuminate the noisy playgrounds.

Therefore, I say to you, young men, however falsely you may deal with your back, be honest with your stomach. Feed well—as well as you can afford to feed. Sleep well. If Benjamin Franklin ever originated the maxim, "six hours of sleep for a man, seven for a woman, and eight for a fool," he ought uniformly to have practised by the rule of the last number. Young man, if you are a student, or engaged in any severe mental occupation, sleep just as long as you can sleep soundly. Lying in bed from laziness is another thing entirely.

Sleep is a thing that bells have no more business to interfere with, than with prayers and sermons. God is re-creating us. We are as unconscious as we were before we were born; and while he holds us there, feeding anew the springs of life, and infusing fresh fire into our brains, and preparing us for the work of another day, the pillow is as sacred as a sanctuary. If any fanatic has made you believe that it is good for you to be violently wakened from your sleep at an early hour, and to go out into the damp, raw air, morning after morning, with your fast unbroken, and your body unfortified by the stimulus of food, forget him and his counsels, and take the full measure of your rest. When you get your breakfast down, take your exercise if you have time, or wait until a later hour in the day. Just as much labor can be accomplished in ten hours as in fourteen, with more efficiency and less fatigue, when rest and bodily exercise are properly taken.

But physical culture—what is that? A very important thing, I assure you. Some of you get this in your employments, and are growing up with manly frames and strong arms. But there are others who are coming up delicately, with spindling shanks, and narrow shoulders, and flat chests, and weak arms—great babies, with soft hands and soft muscles, and not enough of physical prowess to undertake to carry a disputed point with the cook in the kitchen. How a woman ever makes up her mind to love such a man as this is a mystery to me. A feminine man is a masculine monster, and no woman with unperverted instincts can love and marry him. A true woman loves a pair of good strong arms, fastened to a pair of broad shoulders, for they can defend her, provide for her, and—but I wander from my subject.

Physical culture perfects a very important portion of the work which good feeding begins. The best material supplied to the mouth, assimilated by the process of digestion, and carried by the blood to the muscles and all the other structures of the body, is essential; but these organs, when constructed and supplied, need not only thorough training for the development of power and the acquisition of facility, but for the preservation of their harmony and health. God sets all the little children playing for this. He lays the necessity of play upon them, and those restless little fellows that are always sliding, or skating, or wrestling, or running, are all inspired by a divine impulse. Those little brothers of yours who drive you half insane by their noise, who will not sit upon your knee a minute without some fresh twist of their bodies, are discharging their primary Christian duties.

A new world, tossed into space by the Creative Hand, informed with its laws of motion, and set spinning on its axis and careering around its orbit, never stops. It is only the boy who gets lazy as he grows older. God puts him in motion at first, and teaches him to use every physical power he possesses, and he does it faithfully at first. Children who sit still do not live. The mission of play does not cease with childhood. When labor is not capable of doing for you what play has done. and when you have no regular task for your bodily powers, you are to play still. Walking and riding, boxing and fencing, playing ball, pitching quoits, rowing and bowling—all these are as legitimate to the man as the simpler sports are to the boy, and are in a degree essential to his happiness and usefulness.

I should be unjust to the age were I to omit the mention of a special point of "physical culture" which has been long neglected. You find as you come into man's estate, that hair has a tendency to grow upon your face. It is the mark by which God meant that men and women should be distinguished from each other in the crowd. That hair was placed there in infinite wisdom, but your fathers have been cutting it off from their chins in small crops for thirty to fifty years, thus impugning Nature's policy, wasting precious time, drawing a great deal of good blood, creating a great deal of bad, and trying to erase from their faces the difference which was intended to be maintained between them and those of women. If you are a man, and have a beard, wear it. You know it was made to wear. It is enough to make a man with a decent complement of information and a common degree of sensibility (and a handsome beard) deny his kind, to see these smooth-faced men around the streets, and actually showing themselves in female society! Let us have one generation of beards.

LETTER VII.

SOCIAL DUTIES AND PRIVILEGES.

Say, shall my little bark attendant sail,
Pursue the triumph and partake the gale?

POPE.

The primal duties shine aloft like stars;
The charities that soothe, and heal, and bless,
Are scatter'd at the feet of man like flowers.

WORDSWORTH

I PROPOSE in this letter to talk to you concerning your relations to society. Many, and I may say most young men fail for many years to get hold of the idea that they are members of society. They seem to suppose that the social machinery of the world is self-operating. They cast their first ballot with an emotion of pride, perhaps, but are sure to pay their first tax with a groan. They see political organizations in active existence; the parish, and the church, and other important bodies that embrace in some form of society all men, are successfully operated; and yet these young men have no part nor lot in the matter. They do not think of giving a day's time to society. They do not think of giving anything to society. They have an idea that the business of society is to look after them; that they are to be provided for, that seats are to be furnished to them in the churches gratis, that the Lyceum is to be kept up for their amusement—that all social movements whatsoever are to be organized and operated without their aid, and that they exist as legitimate objects of their criticism. This is the very stupidity of selfishness. Some of you haven't known the fact until now, and are not very much to blame. It is one of the incidents of what Fanny Kemble once called your "age of detestability."

One of the first things a young man should do is to see that he is acting his part in society. The earlier this is begun the better. I think that the opponents of secret societies in colleges have failed to estimate the benefit which it must be to every member to be obliged to contribute to the support of his particular organization, and to assume personal care and responsibility as a member. If these societies have a tendency to teach the lesson of which I speak, they are a blessed thing.

Half the ills of society originate in the fact that its burdens are unequally borne, and that the duties of individuals to it are not discharged. Therefore I say to every young man, begin early to do for the social institutions in which you have your life. If you have intellect and accomplishments, give them to the elevation and delight of the circle in which you move. If you have none of these, show an accommodating disposition by attending the sewing circle and holding yarn for the girls. Do your part, and be a man among men. Assume your portion of social responsibility, and see that you discharge it well. If you do not do this, then you are mean, and society has the right to despise you just as much as it chooses. You are, to use a word more emphatic than agreeable, a sneak, and have not a claim upon your neighbors for a single polite word.

Young men have all noticed how easily some of their number get into society, and how others remain out of a good social circle always. They are very apt to think that society has not discharged its duties to them. Now all social duties are reciprocal. Society, as it is called, is far more apt to pay its dues to the individual than the individual to society. Have you, young man, who are at home whining over the fact that you cannot get into society, done anything to give you a claim to social recognition? Are you able to make any return for social recognition and social privileges? Do you know anything? What kind of coin do you propose to pay in the discharge of the obligation which comes upon you with social recognition? In other words, as a return for what you wish to have society do for you, what can you do for society? This is a very important question—more important to you than to society. The question is, whether you will be a member of society by right, or by courtesy. If you have so mean a spirit as to be content to be a beneficiary of society—to receive favors and confer none—you have no business in the society to which you aspire. You are an exacting, conceited fellow.

You ask me what society would have of you. Anything that you possess which has value in society. Society is not particular on this point. Can you act in a charade? Can you dance? Can you tell a story well? Have you travelled, and have you a pleasant faculty of telling your adventures? Are you educated, and able to impart valuable ideas and general information? Have you vivacity in conversation? Can you sing? Can you play whist, and are you willing to assist those to a pleasant evening who are not able to stand through a party? Do you wear a good coat, and can you bring good dress into the ornamental department of society? Are you up to anything in the way of private theatricals? If you do not possess a decent degree of sense, can you talk decent nonsense? Are you a good beau, and are you willing to make yourself useful in waiting on the ladies on all occasions? Have you a good set of teeth, which you are willing to show whenever the wit of the company gets off a good thing? Are you a true, straight-forward, manly fellow, with whose healthful and uncorrupted nature it is good for society to come in contact? In short, do you possess anything of any social value? If you do, and are willing to impart it, society will yield itself to your touch. If you have nothing, then society, as such, owes you nothing. Christian philanthropy may put its arm round you, as a lonely young man, about to spoil for want of something, but it is very sad and humiliating for a young man to be brought to that. There are people who devote themselves to nursing young men, and doing them good. If they invite you to tea, go by all means, and try your hand. If, in the course of the evening, you can prove to them that your society is desirable, you have won a point. Don't be patronized.

Young men are very apt to get into a morbid state of mind, which disinclines them to social intercourse. They become devoted to business with such exclusiveness, that all social intercourse is irksome. They go out to tea as if they were going to jail, and drag themselves to a party as to an execution. This disposition is thoroughly morbid, and to be overcome by going where you are invited, always, and at any sacrifice of feeling. Don't shrink from contact with anything but bad morals. Men who affect your unhealthy mind with antipathy, will prove themselves very frequently to be your best friends and most delightful companions. Because a man seems uncongenial to you, who are squeamish and foolish, you have no right to shun him. We become charitable by knowing men. We learn to love those whom we have despised by rubbing against them. Do you not remember some instance of meeting a man or woman at a watering-place whom you have never previously known nor cared to know—an individual, perhaps, against whom you have entertained the strongest prejudices—but to whom you became bound by a life-long friendship through the influence of a three days' intercourse? Yet if you had not thus met, you would have carried through life the idea that it would be impossible for you to give your fellowship to such an individual.

God has introduced into human character infinite variety, and for you to say that you do not love and will not associate with a man because he is unlike you, is not only foolish but wrong. You are to remember that in the precise manner and degree in which a man differs from you, do you differ from him; and that from his standpoint you are naturally as repulsive to him as he, from your standpoint, is to you. So, leave all this talk of congeniality to silly girls and transcendental dreamers. Do your business in your own way, and concede to every man the privilege which you claim for yourself. The more you mix with men, the less you will be disposed to quarrel, and the more charitable and liberal will you become. The fact that you do not understand a man, is quite as likely to be your fault as his. There are a good many chances in favor of the conclusion that, if you fail to love an individual whose acquaintance you make, it is through your own ignorance and illiberality. So I say, meet every man honestly; seek to know him; and you will find that in those points in which he differs from you rests his power to instruct you, enlarge you, and do you good. Keep your heart open for everybody, and be sure that you shall have your reward. You shall find a jewel under the most uncouth exterior; and associated with omeliest manners and the oddest ways and the ugliest aces, you will find rare virtues, fragrant little humanities, and inspiring heroisms.

Again: you can have no influence unless you are social. A strictly exclusive man is as devoid of influence as an ice-peak is of verdure. If you will take a peep at the Hudson river some bright morning, you will see, ploughing grandly along towards the great metro polis, a magnificent steamer, the silver wave peeling off from her cutwater, and a million jewels sparkling in her wake, passing all inferior barks in sublime indiffer ence, and sending yacht and skiff dancing from her heel. Right behind her, you shall see a smaller steamer, the central motive power of a plateau of barges, loaded to their edges with the produce of thousands of well tilled acres. She has fastened herself to these barges by lines invisible to you. They may be homely things, but they contain the food of the nation. Her own speed may be retarded by this association, but the work she does for commerce is ten fold greater than that accomplished by the grand craft that shuns abrasion as misfortune, and seeks to secure nothing but individual dignity and fast time. It is through social contact and absolute social value alone that you can accomplish any great social good. It is through the invisible lines which you are able to attach to the minds with which you are brought into association alone that you can tow society, with its deeply freighted interests, to the great haven of your hope.

The revenge which society takes upon the man who isolates himself, is as terrible as it is inevitable. The pride which sits alone, and will do nothing for society, because society disgusts it, or because its possessor does not at once have accorded to him his position, will have the privilege of sitting alone in its sublime disgust till it drops into the grave. The world sweeps by the isolated man, carelessly, remorsely, contemptuously. He has no hold upon society, because he is not a part of it. The boat that refuses to pause in its passage, and throw a line to smaller craft, will bring no tow into port. So let me tell you, that if you have an honorable desire in your heart for influence, you must be a thoroughly social man. You cannot move men until you are one of them. They will not follow you until they have heard your voice, shaken your hand, and fully learned your principles and your sympathies. It makes no difference how much you know, or how much you are capable of doing. You may pile accomplishment upon acquisition mountain high; but if you fail to be a social man, demonstrating to society that your lot is with the rest, a little child with a song in its mouth, and a kiss for all, and a pair of innocent hands to lay upon the knees, shall lead more hearts and change the direction of more lives than you.

LETTER VIII.

THE REASONABLENESS AND DESIRABLENESS OF RELIGION.

Greatness and goodness are not means, but ends!
Hath he not always treasures, always friends,
The great good man? Three treasures, love and light,
And calm thoughts, regular as infants' breath;
And three firm friends, more sure than day and night—
Himself, his maker, and the angel death?

COLERIDGE.

YOUNG men, I hate cant, and I do not know exactly how to say what I wish to say in this letter; but I desire to talk to you rationally upon the subject of religion. Now don't stop reading at the mention of this word, but read this letter through. The fact is, it is the most important letter I have undertaken to write to you. I know you, I think, very thoroughly. Life looks so good to you, and you are anticipating so much from it, that religion comes to you, and comes over you like a shadow. You associate it with long faces, and prayer meetings, and psalm-singing, and dull sermons and grave reproofs and stupidity. Your companions are gay, and so are you. Perhaps you make a jest of religion; but deep down in your heart of hearts you know that you are not treating religion fairly. You know perfectly well that there is something in it for you, and that you must have it. You know that the hour will come when you will specially need it. But you wish to put it off, and "enjoy life" first. This results very much from the kind of preaching you have always listened to. You have been taught that human life is a humbug, that these things which so greatly delight you are vain and sinful, that your great business in this world is to be saved, and that you are only to be saved by learning to despise things that you love, and to love things which you despise. You feel that this is unnatural and irrational. I think it is, myself. Now let me talk to you.

Go with me, if you please, to the next station-house, and look off upon that line of railroad. It is as straight as an arrow. Out run the iron lines, glittering in the sun,—out, as far as we can see, until, converging almost to a single thread, they pierce the sky. What were those rails laid in that way for? It is a road, is it?

Try your cart or your coach there. The axletrees are too narrow, and you go bumping along upon the sleepers. Try a wheelbarrow. You cannot keep it on the rail. But that road was made for something. Now go with me to the locomotive shop. What is this? We are told it is a locomotive. What is a locomotive? Why, it is a carriage moved by steam. But it is very heavy. The wheels would sink into a common road to the axle. That locomotive can never run on a common road, and the man is a fool who built it. Strange that men will waste time and money in that way! But stop a moment. Why wouldn't those wheels just fit those rails? We measure them, and then we go to the track and measure its gauge.' That solves the difficulty. Those rails were intended for the locomotive, and the locomotive for the rails. They are good for nothing apart. The locomotive is not even safe anywhere else. If it should get off, after it is once on, it would run into rocks and stumps, and bury itself in sands or swamps beyond recovery.

Young man, you are a locomotive. You are a thing that goes by a power planted inside of you. You are made to go. In fact, considered as a machine, you are very far superior to a locomotive. The maker of the locomotive is man; your maker is man's maker. You are as different from a horse, or an ox, or a camel, as a locomotive is different from a wheelbarrow, a cart, or a coach. Now do you suppose that the being who made you—manufactured your machine, and put into it the motive power—did not make a special road for you to run upon? My idea of religion is that it is a railroad for a human locomotive, and that just so sure as it undertakes to run upon a road adapted only to animal power, will it bury its wheels in the sand, dash itself among rocks, and come to inevitable wreck. If you don't believe this, try the other thing. Here are forty roads: suppose you choose one of them, and see where you come out. Here is the dram-shop road. Try it. Follow it, and see how long it will be before you come to a stump and a smash-up. Here is the road of sensual pleasure. You are just as sure to bury your wheels in the dirt as you try it. Your machine is too heavy for that track altogether. Here is the winding, uncertain path of frivolity. There are morasses on each side of it, and, with the headway that you are under, you will be sure, sooner or later, to pitch into one of them. Here is the road of philosophy, but it runs through a country from which the light of Heaven is shut out; and while you may be able to keep your machine right side up, it will only be by feeling your way along in a clumsy, comfortless kind of style, and with no certainty of ever arriving at the heavenly station-house. Here is the road of scepticism. That is covered with fog, and a fence runs across it within ten rods. Don't you see that your machine was never intended to run on those roads? Don't you *know* that it never was, and don't you know that the only track under heaven upon which it can run safely is the religious track? Don't you know that just as long as you keep your wheels on that track, wreck is impossible? Don't you know that it is the only track on which wreck is not certain? I know it, if you don't; and I tell you that on that track which God has laid down expressly for your soul to run upon, your soul will find free play for all its wheels, and an unobstructed and happy progress. It is straight and narrow, but it is safe and solid, and furnishes the only direct route to the heavenly city. Now, if God made your soul, and made religion for it, you are a fool if you refuse to place yourself on the track. You cannot prosper anywhere else, and your machine will not run anywhere else.

I suppose that a nice casuist would say that I had hus far talked only of morality—only of obedience to law But I was only dealing with the subject in the rough, and trying to show you how rational a thing religion is, and to bring to your comprehension your natural relation to it. I know that the rule of your life is selfishness. I know that you are sinful, polluted, wilful, and that you act from low motives. I know that the race to which you belong have all fallen from innocence, and that they have so thoroughly put out the light that God meant should light every man who comes into the world, that, supplementary to the natural moral system, He has, in great benevolence, devised a scheme of religion, embracing salvation. This is Christianity, and its purpose is to get you back upon the track where the race first started. It is a divine contrivance, or plan, for accomplishing this purpose.

Jesus Christ saw the whole mass of human machinery off the track, and going to irremediable ruin just so truly as he did not interfere to prevent it. He came and told us all how to get back, through repentance, faith, reformation, the surrender of will, the abnegation of self, and the devotion of the heart in love to God and good will to men. He placed himself upon the track and ran over it, not only showing us how to get there ourselves, but showing us how to run when there. In other words, he exhibited to us a true human life. Then, when he had cleared away all the rubbish from the track, shown us how to get upon it again, how to run when we get there, how to avoid and repair accidents by the way,—when he had done all this, and set his agents at work in carrying out his plans, he went back to Heaven, and now looks down to see how the work goes on.

Young men, *I* believe this. I know it is true, and I know, and God knows that this plan which he has devised to save you and make it possible for you to lead a true human life, which shall ultimate in life's highest issues, is the only one which can save you. I know that you can never be happy until you have heartily and practically accepted this religion ; and for you to go on, year after year, carelessly, thoughtlessly, spoiling yourself, growing harder, meaner, more polluted, with no love to God and outgushing benevolence to men, is an insult to Jesus Christ and a brutal wrong to that which he came to save. The fact is that sin is the most unmanly thing in God's world. You never were made for sin and selfishness. You were made for love and obedience. If you think it is manly to reject religion, and the noble obligations it imposes upon you, it only shows how strong a hold the devil has upon you. It shows how degraded you are ; how the beast that is in you domineers over the soul that is in you.

Young man, your personal value depends entirely upon your possession of religion. You are worth to yourself what you are capable of enjoying; you are worth to society the happiness you are capable of imparting. To yourself, without religion, you are worth very little. A man whose aims are low, whose motives are selfish, who has in his heart no adoration for the great God, and no love of his Christ, whose will is not subordinate to the Supreme will—gladly and gratefully—who has no faith, no tenable hope of a happy immortality, no strong-armed trust that with his soul it shall be well in all the future, cannot be worth very much to himself. Neither can such a man be worth very much to society, because he has not that to bestow which society most needs for its prosperity and its happiness. A locomotive off the track is worth nothing to its owner or the public so long as it is off the track. The conditions of its legitimate and highest value are not complied with. It cannot be operated satisfactorily to the owner, or usefully to the public, because it is not where it was intended to run by the man who made it.

Just look at the real object of religion, and see how rational it is. It is the placing of your souls in harmony with God and his laws. God is the perfect, supreme soul, and your souls are the natural offspring of that soul. Your souls are made in the image of his, and, like all created things, are subject to certain immutable laws. The transgression of these laws damages your souls, warps them, stunts their growth, outrages them. Do you not see that you can only be manly and attain a manly growth by preserving your true relations and likeness to the father soul, and a strict obedience to the laws of your being? God has given you appetites, and he meant you should indulge them, and that they should be sources of happiness to you; but always in a way which shall not interfere with your spiritual growth and development. He gave you passions, and they are just as sacred as any part of you, but they are to be under the strict control of your reason and your conscience. He gave you desires for earthly happiness. He planted in you the love of human praise, delight in society, the faculty to enjoy all his works. He gave you his works to enjoy, but you can only enjoy them truly when you regard them as blessings from the great Giver, to feed and not starve your higher natures. There is not a true joy in life which you are required to deprive yourself of, in being faithful to him and his laws. Without obedience to law, your souls cannot be healthful, and it is only to a healthful soul that pleasure comes with its natural—its divine aroma. Is a nose stuffed with drugs capable of perceiving the delicate fragrance of the rose? Is the soul that intensifies its pleasures as an object of life capable of a healthful appreciation of even purely sensual pleasures? The idea of a man's enjoying life without religion is absurd.

I have been thus particular upon this point, because I love you, and because I know that without it, or independent of it, all my previous talk has very littl significance. I have reasoned the thing to you on its merits, and I urge it upon your immediate attention, as a matter of duty and policy. The matter of duty you understand. I do not need to talk to you about that. Now about the policy. It will not be five years, probably, before every one of you will be involved, head and ears, in business. Some of you are thus involved already. You grow hard as you grow older. You get abits of thought and life which incrust you. You ecome surrounded with associations which hold you, o that the longer you live without religion the worse will be for you, and the less probable will be your doption of a religious life. If you expect to be a man, you must begin now. It is so easy, comparatively, to lo it now!

With this paragraph I cease to direct my words particularly to you. What I have said to you, I have said heartily and conscientiously. I shall see you some time. We are none of us to live very long, but if we all act the manly part we were sent here to act, and are true to God and ourselves, we shall be gathered into a great kingdom, whose throne will be occupied by the founder of our religion. During some golden hour of that cloudless day, sitting or straying upon some heavenly hill, watching upon the far-stretching plains the tented hosts of God's redeemed, or marking the shadow of an angel's flight across the bright mirror of the river of life, I shall say something about these letters to you. I shall look you in the face as I say it, to see if you are moved to an emotion of gratitude or of gratification; and if you should happen to tell me that they made you better, that they led you to a higher development, that they directed you to a manly and a godly life, I should press your hand, and if I should keep from weeping it would be more than I can do now.

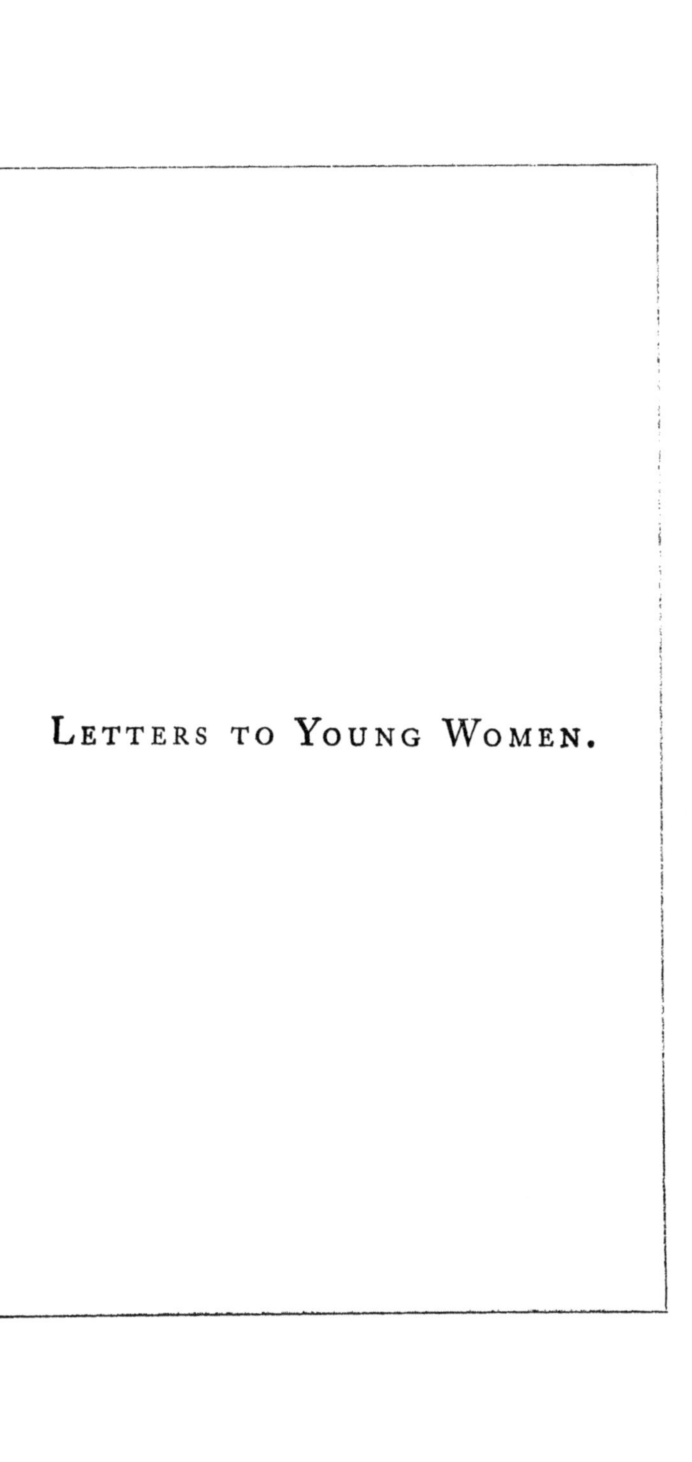

LETTERS TO YOUNG WOMEN.

LETTERS TO YOUNG WOMEN

———o———

LETTER I.

DRESS—ITS PROPRIETIES AND ABUSES.

A creature not too bright or good
For human nature's daily food;
For transient sorrows, simple wiles,
Praise, blame, love, kisses, tears, and smiles.

* * * * * * * *

A perfect woman, nobly planned
To warn, to comfort, and command.

WORDSWORTH.

I have observed, among all nations, that the women ornament themselves more than the men.

JOHN LEDYARD.

I ACCOUNT a pure, beautiful, intelligent, and well-bred woman, the most attractive object of vision and contemplation in the world. As mother, sister, and wife, such a woman is an angel of grace and goodness, and makes a heaven of the home which is sanctified and glorified by her presence. As an element of society she invites into finest demonstrations all that is good in the heart, and shames into secresy and silence all that is unbecoming and despicable. There may be more of greatness and of glory in the higher developments of manhood, but, surely, in womanhood God most delights to show the beauty of the holiness and the sweetness of the love of which he is the infinite source. It is for this reason that a girl or a young woman is a very sacred thing to me. It is for this reason that a silly young woman or a vicious one makes me sigh or shudder. It is for this reason that I pray that I may write worthily to young women.

In getting at a piece of work, it is often necessary, as a preliminary, to clear away rubbish; and I say at first that I do not write to masculine young women. I deem masculine women abnormal women, and I therefore refer all those women who wish to vote, who delight in the public exhibition of themselves, who bemoan the fate which drapes them in petticoats, who quarrel with St. Paul and their lot, who own more rights than they possess; and fail to fulfil the duties of their sphere while seeking for its enlargement—I refer all these to the eight letters recently addressed to young men. They will find some practical remarks in those letters upon masculine development and a manly discharge of life's duties. My theory may be very unsound, but it is my belief, that the first natural division of the human race is marked by the line that distinguishes the sexes. I believe that a true woman is just as different from a true man as a true man is different from a true woman. The nature and the constitution of the masculine are one, and the nature and constitution of the feminine are another. So of the glory attached to each; so of the functions; so of the sphere Therefore, if there be "strong-minded women" who read these letters, I bid them, with all kindness, to turn to the other series for that which will most benefit them.

I shall talk first of that thing which, worthily or most unworthily, engages the minds of all young women, viz.—DRESS. I speak of this first, because it is part of the rubbish which I wish to get out of the way before commencing more serious work; and yet this is not altogether trivial. I believe in dress. I believe that God delights in beautiful things, and as he has never made anything more beautiful than woman, I believe that that mode of dressing the form and face which best harmonizes with their beauty, is that which pleases him best. I believe the mode of female dress prevalent among the Shaker women is absolute desecration. To take anything which infinite ingenuity and power have made beautiful, and capable by the gracefulness of its form and the harmony of its parts of producing the purest pleasure to the observer, and clothe it with a meal bag and crown it with a sugar-scoop, is an irreverent trifling with sacred things which should be punished by mulct and imprisonment.

It is a shame to any woman who has the means to dress well, to dress meanly, and it is a particular shame for any woman to do this in the name of religion. I have seen women who, believing the fashionable devotion to dress to be sinful, as it doubtless is, go to that extreme in plainness of attire which, if it prove anything touching the power that governs them, proves that it is a power which is at war with man's purest instincts, and most elevated tastes. I say it is a shame for a woman to dress unattractively who has it in her power to dress well. It is every woman's duty to make herself pleasant and attractive by such raiment and ornament as shall best accord with the style of beauty with which she is endowed. The beauty of woman's person was intended to be a source of pleasure—the fitting accompaniment of that which in humanity is the most nearly allied to the angelic. Surely, if God plants flowers upon a clod they may rest upon a woman's bosom, or glorify a woman's hair!

But dress is a subordinate thing, because beauty is not the essential thing. Beauty is very desirable; it is a very great blessing; it is a misfortune to possess an unattractive person; but there are multitudes of women with priceless excellences of heart and mind who are not beautiful. Beauty, so far as it is dependent upon form and color, is a material thing, and belongs to the grosser nature. Therefore, dress is a subject which should occupy comparatively few of the thoughts of a true woman, whether beautiful or not. To dress well, becomingly, even richly, if it can be afforded, is a woman's duty. To make the dress of the person the exponent of personal taste, is a woman's privilege. But to make dress the grand object of life; to think of nothing and talk of nothing but that which pertains to the drapery and artificial ornament of the person, is but to transform the trick of a courtesan into amusement for a fool. There are multitudes of women with whom dress is the all-prevalent thought. They think of it, dream of it, live for it. It is enough to disgust one to hear them talk about it. It goes with them from the gaiety of the ball-room into the weeds of the house of death. They use it as a means for splitting grief into vulgar fractions, and are led out from great bereavements into the consolations of vanity, by the hands of numerators and denominators. They flatter one another, envy one another, hate one another—all on the score of dress. They go upon the street to show their dresses. They enter the house of God to display their bonnets. They actually prize themselves more highly for what they wear than for any charm of person or mind which they may possess!

One of the most vulgar and unbecoming things in the world is this devotion to dress, which, in many minds, grows into a form of insanity, and leads to the worship of dry goods and dress-makers. Now it will be impossible for me to give you special directions upon this subject of dress. Your dress-maker and your books, and, better than all, your own taste and experience, will tell you what colors become your complexion, what style of make best accords with your form and style of movement. I shall only speak generally; and I say, first, *dress modestly*. It is all well enough for little girls to show their necks, but for a woman to make her appearance in the society of young men with such displays of person as are made in what is so mistakenly called "full dress," is a shame to her. I know what fashion allows in this matter, and fashion has many sins to answer for. Thousands of girls dress in a manner that they would discard with horror and disgust, if they knew the trains of thought which are suggested by their presence. I know young men, and I know there is not one in one hundred who attends a "full dress party," and comes out as pure and worthy a man as he went in. There is not one in one hundred who does not hold the secret of a base thought suggested by the style of dress which he sees around him. This may tell very badly for young men. Doubtless it does; but we are obliged to take things as we find them. The millennium has not dawned yet, and we have receded to a considerable distance from the era of human innocence. I tell you a fact; and, if you are modest young women, you will heed its suggestions. If you choose to become the objects of foul fancies among young men, whose respect you are desirous of securing, you know the way.

Again, shun peculiarities of dress which attract the attention of the vulgar. Just now the red petticoat is the talk of the newspaper world. It is the inspiring theme of many a sportive pen, and when one of these is seen upon the street, it attracts the attention of the prurient crowd. A modest woman will shun a notoriety like this, until it ceases to be such. I should deprecate the appearance upon the street of a sister of mine with such a garment, ostentatiously displayed, as a calamity to her; and yet I do not believe I am a squeamish man I know that a young woman can dress in such a way as to excite a chaste and worthy admiration among her own sex as well as mine, and my judgment tells me that that is the proper dress for her to wear. I feel that it is right and well for her to dress like this, and that it is not right and well for her to dress otherwise.

Again, dress in such a manner that your attire will not occupy your thoughts after it is upon you. Let every garment be well fitted and well put on—ugly in no point, fussy in no point, nor made of such noticeable material that you necessarily carry with you the consciousness that people around you are examining it. Make it always subordinate to yourself—tributary to your charms, rather than constituent of them. Then the society in which you move will see *you*, and not your housings and trappings. "Jane was dressed very becomingly," or "how well Jane looked," are very much more complimentary comments than "that was a splendid dress that Jane wore;" and a tolerably acute mind may gather from these expressions the philosophy of the whole thing.

There is, as a general thing, no excuse for attire which is not neat and orderly, at any time in the day. A thoroughly neat and orderly young woman is presentable at any hour, whether she be in the kitchen or parlor; and I have seen specimens of womanhood that were as attractive at the wash-tub, with their tidy hair and their nine-penny calico, as in their parlors at a later hour, robed in silk and busy at their embroidery. Materials may be humble, but they may always be tastefully made and neatly kept. There are few habits that a young woman may acquire which, in the long run, will tend more to the preservation of her own self-respect than that of thorough tastefulness, appropriateness, and tidiness of dress, and certainly very few which will make her more agreeable to others.

So, I say, dress well if you can afford it, always neatly, never obtrusively, and always with a modest regard to rational ideas of propriety. Scorn the idea of making dress in any way the great object of life. It is beneath you. A woman was made for something higher than a convenient figure for displaying dry-goods and the possibilities of millinery and mantua-making.

LETTER II.

THE TRANSITION FROM GIRLHOOD TO WOMANHOOD

O mirth and innocence! O milk and water!
Ye happy mixtures of more happy days!

BYRON.

We figure to ourselves the thing we like, and then we build it up as chance will have it, on the rock or sand.

HENRY TAYLOR.

EVERY young woman who has arrived at twenty years of age has passed through three dispensations—the chaotic, the transitional, and the crystalline. The chaotic usually terminates with the adoption of the long skirt. Then commences the transitional dispensation, involving the process of crystallization. This process may go on feebly for years, or it may proceed so rapidly that two years will complete it. In some women, it is never completed, in consequence of a lack of inherent vital force, or a criminal disregard of the requisite conditions. This transitional dispensation, which is better characterized by calling it the silly dispensation, is so full of dangers that it calls for a separate letter; and this I propose to write now.

The silly dispensation or stage of a young woman's life is marked by many curious symptoms, some of them indicative of disease. As the cutting of the natural teeth is usually accompanied by various disorders, so the cutting of the spiritual teeth in women is very apt to exhibit its results in abnormal manifestations. They sometimes eat slate pencils and chalk, and some have been known to take kindly to broken bits of plastering. Others take a literary turn, and, not content with any number of epistles to female acquaintances, send in contributions to the press, which the friendly and appreciative editor kindly and carefully returns, or as kindly and carefully loses, or fails to receive. Others still take to shopping and dawdling with clerks who have dawning beards, red cheeks, and frock coats with outside pockets, from which protrude white handkerchief-tips. Still others yoke themselves in pairs, drawn together by sympathetic attraction, and by community of mental exercise on the subject of beaux. You shall see them walking through the streets, locked arm in arm, plunging into the most charming confidences, or, if you happen to sleep in the house with them, you shall hear them talking in their chamber until, at midnight, the monotonous hum of their voices has soothed you into sleep; and the same voices, with the same unbroken hum, shall greet your ears in the morning. Others take to solitude and long curls. They walk with their eyes down, murmuring to themselves, with the impression that everybody is looking at them.

If a young woman can be safely carried through this dispensation, the great step of life will have been gained. This is the era of hasty marriages, deathless attachments which last until they are superseded, and deliberately formed determinations to live a maiden life, which endure until the reception of an offer of marriage. If, during this period, a young woman be at home, engaged more or less in the duties of the household, or, if she be engaged in study, with the healthful restraints and stimulus of general society about her, it is very well for her. But if she be among her mates constantly, with nothing to do, or if she be shut up in a boarding-school conducted on the high pressure principle, where imagination is stimulated by restraint, and disobedience to law is provoked by its unreasonableness, it is indeed very bad for her.

It is probable that the theatre is a school of vice rather than of virtue, that the ball-room is a promoter of dissipation, and that indiscriminate society has its temptations and its dangers; but a female boarding-school, shut off from general society by law, its members lacking free exercise in the open air, denied the privilege of daily amusements, and presided over by teachers who fail to understand the nature of the precious material they have in charge, is as much worse for mind and morals than all these combined, as can well be imagined. I know female boarding-schools that are properly conducted, whose teachers know what a girl is, and what she needs, and who contrive to lead her through this transitional passage of her life into a healthful and rational womanhood; and I know others whose very atmosphere is that of fever. I know boarding-schools where beaux are the everlasting topic of conversation, and where an unhealthy imagination is so stimulated by irrational restraints and mutual fellow-feeding, that the foundation of nearly every character is necessarily laid in rottenness.

If any young woman, in a boarding-school or out of it, should find herself a subject of any of the diseases which I have pointed out, she should seek a remedy at once. If she finds herself moved to go shopping for the simple purpose of talking with the clerks, let her remember that she is not only doing an immodest and unbecoming thing, but that she is manifesting the symptom of that which is a dangerous mental disease. To begin with, she is doing a very silly thing. Again, she is doing that which compromises her in the eyes of all sensible young men. If she finds herself possessed with unaccountable proclivities to a mineral diet, or a foggy out-reaching for something or other that manifests itself in profound confidences with one similarly afflicted, or any one of a hundred absorbing sentimentalisms, let her remember that she is mentally and morally sick, and that, for her own comfort and peace, she should seek at once for a remedy. Her only safety is in seeking direct contact with a healthier and more advanced life, and by securing healthful occupation for all her powers, intellectual and physical. Dreams, imaginations, silly talk and twaddle about young men, yearnings after sympathetic hearts, the dandling of precious little thoughts about beaux on the knees of fancy, and all that sort of nonsense should be discarded —thrust out of the sacred precincts of the mind—as if they were so many foul reptiles. Get out of this feverish and unhealthy frame just as soon as possible, and walk forth into a more natural, dignified, and womanly life.

A young woman at this age should remember that

her special business is to fit herself for the duties of life. I would not deny to her the society of young men, when she has time for it, and a proper opportunity, but she should remember that she has nothing to do with beaux, nothing to do with thoughts of and calculations for marriage, nothing to do but to become, in the noblest way, a woman. She should remember that she is too young to know her own mind, and that, as a general thing, it is not worth knowing. Girlish attachments and girlish ideas of men are the silliest things in all the world. If you do not believe it, ask your mothers. Ninety-nine times in a hundred they will tell you that they did not marry the boy they fancied, before they had a right to fancy anybody. If you dream of matrimony for amusement, and for the sake of killing time, I have this to say, that, considering the kind of young men you fancy, you can do quite as well by hanging a hat upon a hitching-post, and worshipping it through your chamber window. Besides, it is during this period of unsettled notions and readily shifting attachments that a habit of flirting and a love of it are generated.

I suppose that coquetry, in its legitimate form, is among a woman's charms, and that there is a legitimate sphere for its employment, for, except in rare natures, it is a natural thing with your sex. Nature has ordained that men shall prize most that which shall cost an effort, and while it has designed that you shall at some time give your heart and hand to a worthy man, it has also provided a way for making the priz he seeks an apparently difficult one to win. It is a simple and beautiful provision for enhancing your value in his eyes, so as to make a difficult thing of that which you know to be unspeakably easy. If you hold yourselves cheaply, and meet all advances with open willingness and gladness, the natural result will be that your lover will tire of you. I introduce this subject here, not because I wish to, but because I am compelled to, in order to explain what I have to say upon the habit and love of flirting.

To become a flirt is to metamorphose into a disgusting passion that which by natural constitution is a harmless and useful instinct. This instinct of coquetry, which makes a woman a thing to be won, and which I suppose all women are conscious of possessing in some degree, is not a thing to be cultivated or developed, at all. It should be left to itself, unstimulated and unperverted, and if, in the formative stage of your womanhood, by initiating shallow attachments and heartlessly breaking them, or seeking to make impressions for the sake of securing attentions which are repaid by insult and negligence, you do violence to your nature, you make of yourself a woman whom your own sex despise, and whom all sensible men who do not mean to cheat you with insincerities as mean as yours, are afraid of. They will not love, and they will not trust you. This instinct, then, is not a thing to be harmlessly played with; and I know of few more unhappy and disgusting sights than a girl bringing into her womanhood this passion—harmful alike to herself and others.

The natural and inevitable influence of the devotion of your thoughts—spoken, written, or unexpressed—to beaux and the subject of marriage, while your mind is undergoing a process of crystallization, is to deter that process, to vitiate it, and to make you unworthy in many ways. It is all-important to you at this time to have the counsel of a good, sensible woman, who shall be your senior by at least ten years. She should be a married woman, and, by all means, your mother, unless there be some natural bar to entire communion between you. Do nothing, and give a cherished entertainment to no thoughts which you are unwilling to reveal to this woman. If your companions persist in keeping subjects of this character before your mind, leave them—cut them.

It is necessary that, while your education is actively in progress, your perceptions be kept healthful, and your sentiments unperverted by thoughtless tampering with a subject which you will some time come to know is one of the most serious moment. It spoils a girl to get the idea into her head, that marriage is the chief end of woman, that education is but a preparation for matrimony, and that accomplishments are nothing but contrivances for catching a husband. And now, young woman, whose eye traces these lines, I ask you to decide how much of this letter belongs to you. How are you living? What is the principal subject of your thoughts? I know that I reveal some young women to themselves; and I only fear that they will find themselves so bound to their seductive thoughts and fancies—so dissipated and enervated by them—that they have not mora strength enough left to break away from them.

LETTER III.

ACQUISITIONS AND ACCOMPLISHMENTS.

Show us how divine a thing
A woman may be made.

WORDSWORTH.

IT is a matter of special importance to you that you comprehend and thoroughly appreciate the difference between accomplishments and scientific and literary acquisitions. A woman may have many acquisitions, and no accomplishments, in the usual meaning of that word, and *vice versâ*. As the life of woman goes in this country, these acquisitions perform their most important office in the process by which they are achieved;—that is, the great work which they do for a woman is that of training and disciplining her mind. Many a woman thoroughly learned Algebra at school, with decided advantage to herself, who never makes a practical use of Algebra. She may have been a good Latin or Greek scholar, but, having no important use for her acquisition in practical life, she suffers her knowledge of those languages to fade out. In short, there are very few of her text-books which, in five years after leaving school, she would not be obliged to review with the severest study before she could re-acquire the credit she won in her last examination. A woman may have a pet acquisition which she transforms, by her manner of treatment, into an accomplishment. Botany is thus transformed, not unfrequently, into a very graceful thing.

An accomplishment differs from a science, or a system of truth of any kind, acquired during the process of education, in that it needs to be permanent, and so far as possible perfect, to be of any use to the individual or to society. Music, drawing, conversation, composition, the French language, dancing—all these in America are regarded as accomplishments; yet of fifty women who acquire either of them, or all of them, not more than two retain them.

Miss Georgiana Aurelia Atkins Green was an intimate friend of mine, or, rather, perhaps I should say, her mother's brother boarded my horse, and I bought my meat of her father. It was the determination of Mrs. Green that her daughter should be a finished lady.

During the finishing process I saw but little of her. It occupied three years, and was performed at a fashionable boarding-school, between the ages of fifteen and eighteen, regardless of expense. When she was finished off, she was brought home in triumph, and exhibited on various occasions to crowds of admiring friends. I went one evening to see her. She was really very pretty, and took up her rôle with spirit, and acted it admirably. I saw a portfolio lying upon her piano, and knowing that I was expected to seize upon it at once, I did so, against Miss Green's protestation, which she was expected to make, of course. I found in it various pencil drawings, a crayon head of the infant Samuel, and a terrible shipwreck in India ink. The sketches were not without merit. These were all looked over, and praised, of course. Then came the music. This was some years ago, and the most that I remember is that she played *O Dolce Concento* with the variations, and the Battle of Prague, the latter of which the mother explained to me during its progress. The pieces were cleverly executed, and then I undertook to talk to the young woman. I gathered from her conversation that Mrs. Martinet, the principal of the school where she had been finished, was a lady of "so much style!" that Miss Kittleton of New York was the dearest girl in the school, and that she (Georgiana) and the said Kittleton were such friends that they always dressed alike; and that Miss Kittleton's brother Fred was a magnificent fellow. The last was said with a blush, from the embarrassments of which she escaped gracefully by stating that the old Kittleton was a banker, and rolled in money.

It was easy to see that the parents of this dear girl admired her profoundly. I pitied her and them, and determined, as a matter of duty, that I would show her just how much her accomplishments were worth. I accordingly asked of my wife the favor to invite the whole family to tea, in a quiet way. They all came, on the appointed evening, and after the tea was over, I expressed my delight that there was one young lady in our neighborhood who could do something to elevate the tone of our society. I then drew out, in a careless way, a letter I had just received from a Frenchman, and asked of Miss Georgiana the favor to read it to me. She took the letter, blushed, went half through the first line correctly, then broke down on a simple word, and confessed that she could not read it. It was a little cruel; but I wished to do her good, and proceeded with my experiment. I took up a piece of music, and asked her if she had seen it. She had not. I told her there was a pleasure in store for both of us. I had heard the song once, and I would try to sing it if she would play the accompaniment. She declared she could not do it without practice, but I told her she was too modest by half. So I dragged her, protesting, to the piano. She knew she should break down. I knew she would, and she did. Well, I would not let her rise, for as Mr. and Mrs. Green were fond of the old-fashioned church music and had been singers in their day, and in their way, I selected an old tune, and called them to the piano to assist. Miss Green gave us the key, and we started off in fine style. It was a race to see which would come out ahead. Georgiana won, by skipping most of the notes. She rose from the piano with her cheeks as red as a beet.

"By the way," said I, "Georgiana, your teacher of drawing must have been an excellent one." I did not tell her that I had seen evidence of this in her own efforts in art, but I touched the right spring, and the lady gave me the teacher's credentials, and told me what such and such people had said of her. "Well," said I, "I am glad if there is one young woman who has learned drawing properly. Now you have nothing to do but to practise your delightful art, and you must do something for the benefit of your friends. I promised a sketch of my house to a particular friend, at a distance, and you shall come up to-morrow and make one. I remember that beautiful cottage among your sketches; and I should prize a sketch of my own, even half as well done, very highly." The poor girl was blushing again, and from the troubled countenances of her parents, I saw that they had begun indistinctly to comprehend the shallowness—the absolute worthlessness—of the accomplishments that had cost them so much. Georgiana acknowledged that she had never sketched from nature—that her teacher had never required it of her, and that she had no confidence that she could sketch so simple an object as my house. The Greens took an early leave, and I regret to say a cool one. They were mortified, and there was not good sense enough in the girl to make an improvement of the hints I had given her.

The Green family resided upon a street that I always took on my way to the post-office, and there was rarely a pleasant evening that did not show their parlor alight, and company within it. I heard the same old variations of *O Dolce Concento* evening after evening. The Battle of Prague was fought over and over again. The portfolio of drawings (such of them as had not been expensively framed) was exhibited, I doubt not, to admiring friends until they were soiled with thumbing. At last, Georgiana was engaged, and then she was married—married to a very good fellow, too. He loved music, loved painting, and loved his wife. Two years passed away; and I determined to ascertain how the pair got along. She was the mother of a fine boy whom I knew she would be glad to have me see. I called, was treated cordially, and saw the identical old portfolio, on the identical old piano. I asked the favor of a tune. The husband with a sigh informed me that Georgiana had dropped her music. I looked about the walls, and saw the crayon Samuel, and the awful shipwreck in India ink. Alas! the echoes of the Battle of Prague that came back over the field of memory, and these fading mementoes around me, were all that remained of the accomplishments of the late Miss Georgiana Aurelia Atkins Green.

Now, young woman, I think you will not need any assurance from me that I have drawn a genuine portrait, for which any number of your acquaintances may have played the original. What do you think of accomplishments like these? How much do they amount to? My opinion of them is that they are the shabbiest of all things that can be associated with a woman's life and history. I have told you this story in order to show you the importance of incorporating your accomplishments with your very life. It is comparatively an easy task to learn a few tunes by rote; to get up, with the assistance of a teacher, a few drawings; to go through with a few French exercises; but it is not so easy to learn the science of music, and go through the manual practice necessary to make the science available under all circumstances. It is not easy to sketch with facility from nature. It is not easy to comprehend the genius of the French language, and so to familiarize yourself with it that it shall ever remain an open language to you, and give you a key to a new literature. A true accomplishment is won only by hard work; but when it is won, it is a part of you, which nothing but your own neglect can take away from you.

And now let me tell you a secret. Multitudes of married men are led to seek the society of other women, or go out among their own fellows, and often into bad habits, because they have drunk every sweet of life which their wives can give them. They have heard all their tunes, seen all their efforts at art, sounded their minds, and measured every charm, and they see that henceforth there is nothing in the society of their wives but insipidity. They married women of accomplishments, but they see never a new development—no improvement. Their wives can do absolutely nothing The shell is broken; the egg is eaten.

The first accomplishment that I would urge upon you, is that of using the English language with correctness, elegance, and facility. There are, comparatively, few young women who can write a good note. *I know of hardly one who can punctuate her sentences* properly. I beg of you never to write affection with a single *f*, or friendship without an *i* in the first syllable. Such slips destroy the words, and the sentiments they represent. If you accomplish yourselves in nothing else, learn thoroughly how to use your mother tongue I remember one young woman with whom, when in youth, I had the misfortune to correspond. In the barrenness of subjects upon which to engage her pen, she once inquired by note whether I ever saw such "a spell of wether," as we had been having. I frankly informed her that I never did, and that I hoped she would never indulge in such another, for it made me cool. She took the hint, and broke off the correspondence.

There are many who can write tolerably well, but who cannot talk. Conversation I am inclined to rank among the greatest accomplishments and the greatest arts. Natural aptness has much to do with this, but no woman can talk well who has not a good stock of definite information. I may add to this, that no woman talks well and satisfactorily who reads for the simple purpose of talking. There must exist a genuine interest in the affairs which most concern all men and women. The book, magazine, and newspaper literature of the time, questions of public moment, all matters and movements relating to art, affairs of local interest —all these a woman may know something of, and know something definitely. Of all these she can talk if she will try, because there is something in all which excites feeling of some kind, and shapes itself into opinion.

But whatever accomplishment a young woman attempts to acquire, let her by all means acquire it thoroughly and keep it bright. Accomplishments all occupy the field of the arts. They are things which have no significance or value save in the ability of doing. They become, or should become, the exponents of a woman's highest personality. They are her most graceful forms of self-expression, and into them she can pour the stream of her thoughts and fancies, and through them utter the highest language of her nature and her culture. Accomplishments make a woman valuable to herself. They greatly increase her pleasure, both directly in the practice, and indirectly through the pleasures which she gives to society. A truly accomplished woman—one whose thoughts have come naturally to flow out in artistic forms, whether through the instrumentality of her tongue, her pen, her pencil, or her piano, is a treasure to herself and to society. Such a woman as this would I have you to be. There may be something to interfere with your being all this; but this you can do: you can acquire thoroughly every accomplishment for which you have a natural aptitude, or you can let it alone. Do not be content with a smattering of anything. Do not be content to play parrot to your teachers, until your lesson is learned, and then think you are accomplished. Do not be content with mediocrity in any accomplishment you undertake. Do not be content to be a Miss Georgiana Aurelia Atkins Green

LETTER IV.

UNREASONABLE AND INJURIOUS RESTRAINTS.

Let me not to the marriage of true minds
Admit impediments.

SHAKSPERE.

I SUPPOSE that most men have observed the following facts, from which I propose to draw a lesson :—First, that young married women have a peculiar charm for unmarried young men, and that a young man's first love is almost uniformly devoted to a woman older than himself.

A marriageable young woman occupies, or is made to occupy, a position of peculiar hardship. Our theory is that a woman should never make an advance towards the man she loves and would marry. Such a step is deemed inconsistent with maiden modesty. I do not quarrel with this, but the effect has been to make young women, who possess sensitive natures, hypocrites. It ought not to do it, but it does. Every modest young woman, possessing a good degree of sagacity, plays a part, almost always, when in the society of young men. The fear is that by some word, or look, or act, she shall express such a degree of interest in a young man as shall lead him to believe that she is after him. Young women study the effect of their language, they often shun civilities, they put on an artificial and constrained style of behavior, for fear that some complacent fool will misconstrue them, or some gentleman whom they wish to please will deem them too forward, and so become disgusted. The result is, that a man rarely finds out either the best or the worst points of his wife's character before he marries her. Social intercourse is carried on under a kind of protest, which places every young woman in a position absolutely false before the eyes of young men. Many a woman owes a life of celibacy and disappointment to the fact that she never felt at liberty to act out herself.

With these statements, it is very easy to understand the attractions which a young married woman has for a bachelor, and to explain the phenomenon of a young man falling in love with a woman older than himself. In the first instance, a married woman becomes agreeable because she becomes perfectly natural and unconstrained, her circumstances allowing all the more grateful forms of politeness—the cordial greeting, the complimentary attentions, and the free conversation—without the danger of being misconstrued. In the latter instance, the woman throws off her constraint in the same manner, because she is in the society of one whom she regards as, in reality, a boy. She finds, very much to her surprise, that she has won the boy's heart; but it was the most natural thing in the world. He had never had a sight of a woman's nature before. The girls with whom he had associated had always worn a mask. The real hearts behind it he had thus far failed to apprehend. There is a very general impression among the young men whose affections are not engaged that the best women are married, and that those who are left do not amount to much. They will think differently some time or other.

Now my idea is that this universal mask-wearing system should be broken up. It does injustice to all parties. If there is, in society, any poor creature in the form of a man whose vanity is so open to flattery that a young woman cannot treat him with natural, cordial politeness, without his thinking that she would like to marry him, and is trying to ensnare him, let him think so, and trust to time and circumstances for justice.

Such men are of too little account in the world to pay for carrying a deceitful face, and despoiling the intercourse of the young of its sweetest charms. If you like the society of young men, take no pains to conceal it, but treat them with frank cordiality. No true gentleman among them will misconstrue you. It is not necessary for you to tell them that you calculate to live a maiden life. They know you lie. It will not do to indicate to any man of sense that you do not like the attentions and society of gentlemen, for he knows better. He knows, at least, that you ought to like them, and that if you do not, there is something wrong about you. Don't practise deception of any kind. A man who is frank and open-hearted with you, deserves to be met with a frank and open heart by you; and in ninety-nine cases in every hundred, men will be honorable and manly with you, if you will lay aside suspicion, and trust them. If a man prove himself unworthy of your confidence, you have your remedy. Cut him, or tell him what you think of him, and bring him upon his knees.

I have given my advice without many qualifications, but do not misconstrue me. I write upon the supposition that you have common sense, and know what I mean. Some people, I suppose, would present you with a formula by which to conduct all your intercourse with young men. I know a large number of fathers and mothers who will think that, upon this subject, I ought to guard my language, and be more particular; but I know very well that if you have not sense and prudence enough to take this general counsel, and use it judiciously, no qualifications that I could make would be of any service to you.

I trust *you.* I believe you are virtuous young women, with pure hearts and true intentions; and I know there is no danger to you until you cease to be such. You have an instinct—God's word in your own souls—that tells you when a man takes the first wrong step towards you; and if you do not repel that step in such a manner that it will never be repeated, do you suppose that anything I could say to you would do you any good? I say this: that perfect frankness and cordiality in the treatment of young men are entirely consistent with the safety of any true woman from insult or offensive familiarity. Is your father afraid to trust you out of his sight? I am not. If I were, I would be ashamed to confess it, particularly if you were a daughter of mine. I believe in you, and I believe, moreover, that if this contemptible idea that men are your natural enemies, and that you must cheat them and look out for them, could be got out of the way, and a free and unconstrained social intercourse established between you and them, they would be much better, and you altogether safer for it.

There is another subject, more or less intimately associated with this, which may as well be treated here. It is very natural for young women to get in the habit of treating only those young men politely whom they happen, for various reasons, to fancy. They "don't care" what the majority of young men think of them, provided they retain the good will of their particular pets. They are whimsical, and take on special and strong likes or dislikes for the young men whom they meet. One is "perfectly hateful," and another is "perfectly splendid," and so they proceed to make fools of themselves over both parties. Now there is nothing upon which a young man is so sensitive as this matter of being treated with polite consideration by the young women of his acquaintance; and I know of nothing which will tend more certainly to make a young man hateful than to treat him as if he were so. There is a multitude of young men whose self-respect is nurtured, whose ambition is quickened, and whose hearts are warmed with a genial fire, by those considerate recognitions on the part of their female acquaintances which assure them that they have a position in the esteem of those with whom they associate the sweetest hopes and happiness of life. To be cut for no good cause is to receive a wound which is not easily healed.

The duty, therefore, which I would inculcate is that

of systematic politeness. If you know a young man, bow to him when you meet him. He will not bow to you first, for he waits for your recognition. He does not know whether you esteem him of sufficient value to be recognised. If you pass him without a recognition, you say to him, in a language which he feels with a keenness which you cannot measure, that you consider him beneath your notice. You plant in his heart immediately a prejudice against yourself. You disturb him. You hurt him, and this, too, let me admit, very frequently without design. You are sensitive yourself, and are afraid he has forgotten you. You think, perhaps, that he would not like to notice you, and would not like to have you notice him. There is a good deal of this kind of thing, doubtless, but it is all wrong. There is no man who will not return your bow, and feel the better for your smile; and if the young man receiving the attention is poor, and has his position in the world to win, and feels that he has not as many attractions, personal or circumstantial, as others, you have made his heart light, and awakened towards yourself a feeling of cordial good will, akin in many instances to gratitude.

A young woman who is afraid of compromising her position by recognising men out of her set, or out of a certain line of genteel occupations, shows by how frail a tenure she holds her own respectability. I could name to you women who have not only a recognised but a commanding position in the best society, who are as uniformly and systematically polite to the clerk who sells them silks, as to the pets of their circle; who have a bow and a smile for all with whom they have ever been thrown into personal relations, and who, by this very politeness, more than by any other self-expression, vindicate their place among those whom society calls ladies. There is a kind word for them in every young man's mouth: and no young man would ever think of presuming upon such politenesses for the indulgence of an offensive familiarity. Such women have a sacredness in his eyes that no other women possess, and he would offend them in no way, for the world.

The advice I have given you in these matters is partly for the benefit of your sex, and partly for mine. I believe that there should be a far more rational mode of intercourse between young men and young women than at present exists. I believe that every legitimate attraction that your society has for young men should be free and unconstrained. I believe that there is no good reason why a young married woman should be more attractive to a bachelor than yourselves, and that in the degree in which they are more attractive, do you wrong yourselves and the young men of your acquaintance. I believe that it is well for you, and well for young men, that they should be attracted to you by a frank behavior on your part, which will place them at their ease, and exercise upon them all that good influence which a pure, strong, outspoken female nature is so well calculated to exert.

Young men and young women, to use a cant phrase of the day, are "in the same boat." But a few years will pass away before they will be the bosom companions of each other, and the fathers and mothers of the land. It matters everything to them that they understand each other; and to this end, in my judgment, an intercourse between them should be established upon a very different basis from that which is now maintained by society. It should be more simple, more ample, more natural, more trustful, and more heartily considerate. There is nothing in the history of the race to prove that anything has ever been preserved or won to virtue by a system of essential falsehood, or a policy of arbitrary constraint. Many a girl feels this, and will feel it to her dying day. To tie a young woman up to the meanly cautious conventionalisms of the day, is to prepare her as a helpless sacrifice to the first designing villain who insinuates himself into her confidence. Many a woman groans to-day in bondage to a drunkard, a libertine, or a dolt, who only needed to have been allowed to know men better to have secured a proper companion.

I say, then, to you, young women, reform this thing altogether. It is in your hands. I give you the idea: I leave you to carry it into practice. You do not need that I should tell you how to do it. If you are not vicious, there is nothing for you, in your mind and heart, to conceal. Be simply yourselves, taking all possible care to make yourselves what you should be. Learn to think kindly of all young men, save those who you have reason to believe possess black hearts and foul intentions—those who are enemies of your sex and social purity. Treat every young man well, both for his sake and your own. You shall thus be the light of many eyes, and your kind heart, thorough good manners, and transparent nature, cannot fail to attract to you those whose true nobility is the most strongly touched by that which is best in womanhood. One of those will become your companion, I am inclined to think, if human nature, meanwhile, do not suffer some remarkable change.

LETTER V.

THE CLAIMS OF LOVE AND LUCRE.

> Maidens, like moths, are ever caught by glare,
> And Mammon wins his way where Seraphs might despair.
>
> BYRON.

YOU calculate when you are married to be married to the man you love, and no other; yet there are a good many chances that you will be influenced in your choice by other considerations. But you should never think of marrying a man simply because you love him. You may love a man who has personal habits that will make you miserable. You may love a man so lazy or so inefficient that your whole life will be necessarily a continued struggle with poverty. You may love a man who has no adaptation to you—who is surly and stupid and unresponsive; who can give no satisfac tory return of your affection, and who will repulse every demonstration of your fondness. You may love a man who is supremely selfish. When you become bound for life to a man, he should be one who can make you happier than you would be alone. There are doubtless some instances of a love so noble and so self-sacrificing that it will welcome poverty and want, with the object of its desire, as being far better than riches without it. I will not quarrel with this. I only say that, generally, competence (I do not mean wealth) is necessary to that degree of comfort without which love fails of its sweetest exercises and most grateful rewards. Love for a man is only one reason why you should marry him. There may be a round dozen of reasons why you should not.

A woman's heart is a very queer thing, on the whole. It falls in love in the most unaccountable way, with the most unaccountable men. It is a hard thing to reason with, and a much harder thing to reason about, yet there are some things which may be said to those whose judgment is not yet blinded by a passion that contemns reason. You should marry a man to whom you will be willing to bend, or one whom you know you can manage without his knowledge, or with his consent. The instances are very rare in which two strong wills can harmonize in close companionship. They must both be governed by principle, and be mutually forbearing from principle. I have seen noble instances of this, but not often. The law of nature is that the wife shall bend to the husband—that her will shall, at last, be subject; yet there are instances of true affection between man and woman when subjection on the part of the man becomes the law of nature, the woman's judgment being the best, and her will the strongest. In these cases, the female mind possesses masculine characteristics and the male mind feminine characteristics; and it is just as proper that her mind should govern in these instances as that the male mind should govern in others. But there is something unnatural in this, after all—or something, I should say, out of the common order of things.

If a woman sincerely believe that there is no man to whose will she can gladly subordinate her own, let her seek out a feminine man, and make suit for his hand. A noted female vocalist, whom all of us love, had the credit of doing this. He gave up even his religion for her, though that may not have cost him much. I presume that she governs him, and I have yet to learn that the union is not thoroughly a happy one. After all, if the lady were a graceful subject of a kingly intellect, I cannot help thinking that she would be in a more natural position, and one in which she would be happier than she is now.

You are placed in a position of peculiar temptation. You have ambitions to be something more than pretty, accomplished, and loved—at least, some of you have. You want a career. As a woman, you see that yo cannot have one, save through a matrimonial connexion You wish to do something—to be something—to be mistress of an establishment, or to be associated with one who has the public eye, or the public consideration. It is thus that wealth and position come to you with very great temptations. A man of wealth or a man of power offers you his hand, and, unless he is absolutely repulsive, he will generally get it. You will try to love him, or learn to love him, or think you love him; or perhaps you will take a mercenary or a worldly view of the whole thing, and marry him for what of wealth and position he can bring you. Now all this marrying for money, or for position, or for any other consideration, when genuine love is absent, is essential prostitution. I know of no difference between selling one's self for a lifetime, and that sale of the soul and body which is made in the house of her whose steps take hold on hel' If you find yourself willing to give up yourself to a m in a life-long connexion for the house he gives you, for the silks and furs with which he clothes you, for the society into which he introduces you, for the position with which he endows you, then, whether you know it or not, you become the sister of the drab whom you so inconsistently spurn from your side. In fact, the motives that have made her what she is may be white by the side of yours. Marrying for love may seem to be a very silly thing to a woman of the world; but marrying without love, for a consideration, is wicked. "Love in a cottage" is laughed at by very "judicious people," but it is a very sweet thing by the side of indifference in a palace. I know of nothing more disgusting in all the world than that mercenary tie which, under the name of marriage, binds a woman to the bosom of one who bought her with his money.

I know what the world says about this matter, and I very heartily despise the world for it. When I ask the world if Jane has "made out well" by her union, and am told that she has done finely, and married a man worth a hundred thousand dollars, I am tempted to be profane. When I ask the world how Kate has settled, and am informed, as the essential portion of the reply, that her husband is "an excellent provider," I am tempted to spit in its face. The conventional idea of a happy and proper matrimonial connexion is so mean and so arbitrary, that it is no wonder that unsophisticated girls sacrifice themselves. I pity them from the bottom of my heart. *They cannot have even the reputation of marrying well unless they allow base motives to enter into their calculations.* They learn early to aim at wealth or position as primary and supremely desirable things. A brilliant match, in the eyes of the world, atones for low morals, uncongenial tastes, and lukewarm hearts.

Now, if you must make calculations, let me help you. Make genuine affection the first thing. This is absolutely indispensable. It takes precedence of everything else. You are not at liberty to consider anything before this. A union based upon anything else, is, as I have already told you, essential prostitution. It is against nature—against God's most wise and benevolent intentions. You can make no union with a man, not based on this, that will give you happiness. Friendship alone will not do. Esteem alone will not do. The idea of giving yourself to a man simply because you esteem him, and respect him, is disgusting. The union of the current of your life with that of a man is the great event of your history, and if this be not through those natural affinities, sympathies, and partialities—that passion of your soul which heaven intended should be called into exercise by manhood—then is it only a conventional union, and no union in fact. Love, then, I say, is the essential thing, and yet love, as I have said before, is only one thing. There may be in the man who excites the holiest and strongest passion of your nature many things which, if you value peace—if you value your own purity, even—should lead you to pluck that passion from your breast, and turn your back upon its object, that God's light may rest upon your brow even if sorrow make darkness in your heart.

It is hard to examine character, and profit by the study, after the heart has become the seat of an absorbing passion; but it is indispensably necessary to do it sometimes. It is far better that the passion be excited by the influence of character, disposition, and bearing, but when study becomes necessary, it should be entered upon conscientiously; for the second requisite for a happy union is sound character. A woman possessing the best elements of womanhood cannot be happy with a man who has not a sound character. He may have a good disposition, he may be intelligent, he may have wealth and honor, but if his character be weak or faulty, she has no reliance; and she must ultimately lose her respect for him. When respect is gone, she may love, she may pity, she may forgive, but she cannot be happy Disposition comes in for consideration in the third place, and worldly circumstances in the fourth, or perhaps still lower in the scale. I might speak of another thing, requisite to happiness in the highest degree, but I will not, now and here.

In the consideration of worldly circumstances, be

wise. Remember that if your lover be intelligent, healthy, the master of a business or a profession, he stands many more chances to die in the possession of wealth or competence than he would if rich now, and without a settled business and settled purposes. I hav watched the results of many matches, and I have seen ten which started with a fortune to be acquired, turn out well in a worldly point of view, where I have seen one result happily, starting with the fortune made. If a young man is honorable, intelligent, industrious, and manly in every respect, and you love him, marry him. There is no power under heaven that has a moral right to stand between you and your happiness. Many a poor girl who married for money now pines in poverty, and covets the position of girls whose wiser choice she once contemned.

I speak in this way for two reasons. The first is, that it is not only your right but your duty to consider whether a life of certain poverty will be compensated by a life of association with the man you love. The second is, that when you take this matter into consideration you should make your judgment upon a sound basis. Wealth in hand, without business habits, business tastes, and business interests, is the most unreliable thing in the world. It may even spoil a good lover, and in time transform him into a loafer or a sot. On the contrary, good business habits, good character, enterprise, ambition—all these combined—are almost sure to secure competence and success. If you would rely on anything, rely on these, for they are the only reliable things. Misfortune may deal harshly with these, but that is the business of Providence.

I fancy one reply that may be made to all this wise talk. Women practically have comparatively little choice in the matter. They grow up from the cradle with the idea that it is a horrible thing to live and die an old maid. That, in the minds of half the girls, is the most terrible thing in all the world. They can abide anything better than that. So they feel a kind of obligation to jump at the first offer, they are so much afraid they shall never have another. Let them remember that a mismated match is much worse than an unmated life. I believe that marriage is the true condition, and that no man or woman can fully enjoy life unmarried; but I know they will be more unhappy if they are badly matched than if not matched at all. But women have more choice than they think, and would have still more than they do, if their intercourse with young men were placed upon the basis indicated in my last letter.

Most young women study the character of men but little, because they have but little opportunity. They see comparatively few, and, through the character of their intercourse, know them very incompletely. It is a sin and a shame that young women enjoy such inferior opportunities of learning the character of young men,—of weighing, comparing, and judging them. It is a shame that they have no more opportunities for a choice. My own wife very fortunately got an excellent husband, but it is something for which she is to be grateful to an overruling Providence, for her own knowledge had very little to do with it. I could have cheated her beyond all account. I tell you, men want studying for some years, before you find them out, and it becomes you to run fewer risks than the most of your sex run in this business. It is a good deal of a step—this getting married, and I am very anxious that you shall know a great many men, that you shall get the one you love, that he shall be worthy of you, and that you shall be happy all the days of your life.

LETTER VI.

THE PRUDENT AND PROPER USE OF LANGUAGE.

Of all the griefs that harass the distressed,
Sure the most bitter is a scornful jest.

SAMUEL JOHNSON.

And lovelier things have mercy shown
To every failing but their own,
And every woe a tear can claim
Except an erring sister's shame.

BYRON.

I HAVE met with a good many young women, first and last, whose intellects were of that keen, quick variety which delights in uttering sharp things—often very hard things. They do it, at first, playfully; they produce a laugh which flatters them; and they soon get to doing it wantonly. They acquire an appetite for praise, and they become willing to procure it at whatever expense to others. Genuine wit in a man is almost always genial; wit in a woman, however genial it may be at first, almost always gets into personalities, sooner or later, which makes it very dangerous and very hateful. Man is held in restraint, whatever his tendencies may be, by the consideration that, as a man, he will be held responsible for his words; women presume upon the fact that they are women, in taking license to say what they choose of each other, and of men in particular. There is not always—perhaps there is not generally—malice in these sharp and hard speeches, but they poison, nevertheless. They poison her who utters them, and they poison those who suffer from them. The utterer becomes the student, for a purpose, of the weak points of her friends, and they learn to hate her. I have known not a few women whose personal witticisms were enjoyed by the gossip-loving crowd around her, every man of whom would as soon think of marrying a tigress as the one he was flattering by the applause of his laugh.

Therefore I say that to be a witty woman is a very dangerous thing. To be a witty woman is to be the subject of very great temptations, for personality forms the very zest of gossip—an employment of which most women, I think, know something by experiment. Men are afraid of witty women, especially those who delight in making cutting speeches. They say, very rationallv, that if a woman will secure praise at the expense of one friend, she will also at the expense of others, and that no one can be safe. There is nothing in my eyes more admirable in a woman than an honest wish to hear no one spoken against—than that consideration for the feelings of others which leads her to treat all faults with tenderness, and all weaknesses and natural unpleasant peculiarities with indulgence. One of the most attractive sights in the world, to any young man of common sensibility, is that of a young woman who not only will neither say nor hear ill of any one, but who takes special pains to notice those whom the crowd neglect. Such a woman is the admired of all whose admiration is worth securing. And now, young woman, if you are one of the sharp ones, and are tempted to say sharp things, remember that you are in very great danger of injuring yourself, not only in your own soul, but in the eyes of all those whom you imagine you are pleasing.

I think, as a general thing, that women are harder in their judgments of their own sex than men are of theirs or even of them. This arises partly from jealousy—a wish to stand among the uppermost in the popular esteem. The praise of women, poured into the ears of other women, is not usually gratefully received. The disposition of women to judge harshly of each other is seen particularly in those instances in which a woman has taken a false step. Here the fact is patent;—a woman forgets, or forgives, much less promptly than a man. However deep the repentance, however decided the reformation, a woman never forgets that her sister has sinned, notwithstanding the fact that weakness and misfortune and a hundred mitigating if not exculpating circumstances plead in her behalf. It is the same with less important lapses of behavior, in a corresponding degree. I do not know but this is one of the safeguards which God intended should be around a woman's path, but it seems to me a very unwomanly and a very unchristian thing. It seems to me, too, to be a very unnatural thing. I judge that, much more than a man, a woman should be interested in securing justice for her own sex; and that if a sinning or a silly woman should find a charitable defender anywhere, it should be among those who, like her, are exposed to the temptations, and particularly to the uncharitable misconstructions, of a captious world.

What I would insist upon, is, that you not only do not wound the feelings of your own sex by sharp criticisms, but that you be heartily enlisted in maintaining their honor. Do not think that you do this while putting down this one and that, in order to make your own immaculateness the more conspicuous. Believe what is generally true, that those who sin are those who sin rather through weakness than vicious tendency; that villains who wear cravats and waistcoats—the very men whom you are by no means particular enough to exclude from your company—are those who most deserve you reproaches

And now that I am upon this subject of talk, it will be well to say all I have to say upon it. It is a very common thing for young women to indulge in hyperbole. A pretty dress is very apt to be "perfectly splendid;" a disagreeable person is too often "perfectly hateful;" a party in which the company enjoyed themselves, somehow becomes transmuted into the "most delightful thing ever seen." A young man of respectable parts and manly bearing is very often "such a magnificent fellow!" The adjective "perfect," that stands so much alone as never to have the privilege of help from comparatives and superlatives, is sadly over-worked, in company with several others of the intense and extravagant order. The result is that, by the use of such language as this, your opinion soon becomes valueless.

A woman who deals only in superlatives demonstrate. at once the fact that her judgment is subordinate to her feelings, and that her opinions are entirely unreliable. All language thus loses its power and significance. The same words are brought into use to describe a ribbon in a milliner's window, as are employed in the endeavor to do justice to Thalberg's execution of Beethoven's most heavenly symphony. The use of hyperbole is so common among women that a woman's criticism is generally without value. Let me insist upon this thing. Be more economical in the use of your mother tongue. Apply your terms of praise with precision; use epithets with some degree of judgment and fitness. Do not waste your best and highest words upon inferior objects, and find that when you have met with something which really is superlatively great and good, the terms by which you would distinguish it have all been thrown away upon inferior things—that you are bankrupt in expression. If a thing is simply good, say so; if pretty, say so; if very pretty, say so; if fine, say so; if very fine, say so; if grand, say so; if sublime, say so; if magnificent, say so; if splendid, say so. These words all have different meanings, and you may say them all of as many different objects, and not use the word "perfect" once. That is a very large word. You will probably be obliged to save it for application to the Deity, or to his works, or to that serene rest which remains for those who love him.

Young women are very apt to imbibe another bad habit, namely, the use of slang. I was walking along the street the other day when I met an elegantly dressed lady and gentleman upon the sidewalk. My attention was the more attracted to them because they were evidently strangers. At any rate they impressed me as being very thoroughly refined and genteel people. As I came within hearing of their voices—they were quietly chatting along the way—I heard these words from the woman's lips: "You may bet your life on that." I was disgusted I could almost have boxed her ears. I remember once being in the company of a belle—one who had had a winter's reign in Washington. Some kind of game was in progress, when, in a moment of surprise, she exclaimed, "My Gracious!" Now you may regard this as a finical notion, but I tell you that woman fell as flatly in my esteem as if she had uttered an oath. A lady, fresh from Paris, once informed me that it would do the residents of a certain quiet village a great deal of good to be "stirred up with a long pole." Let us see how you like this kind of talk.

If you wish to be an "A No. 1" woman, you have got to "toe the mark," and be less "hifalutin." "You may bet your head on that." You may sing "slightually" "like a martingale," you may "spin street yarn" at the rate of ten knots an hour, you may "talk like a book," you may dance as if you were on "a regular break-down," you may "turn up your nose at common folks," and play the piano "mighty fine," but "*I-tell-you*," you "can't come to tea." "You may be hand some, but you can't come in." You might just as well "cave in," first as last, and "absquatulate," for you can't "put it through," "any way you can fix it." If you imagine that you may "go it while you are young, for when you are old you can't," you won't "come it," "by a long chalk." "Own up," now, and "do the straight thing," and I'll "set you down" as "one of the women we read of." If you can't "come up to the scratch," why I must "let you slide." But if you have a "sneakin' notion" for being a "regular brick," there is no other way—"not as you knows on"—"no sir-ree-hoss?" If a young man should "kind o' shine up to you," and you should "cotton to him," and he should hear you say "by the jumping Moses," or "by the living jingo," or "my goodness," or "I vow," or "go it, Betsey, I'll hold your bonnet," or "mind your eye," or "hit 'im agin," or "take me away," or "dry-up, now," or "draw your sled," or "cut stick," or "give him particular fits," he would pretty certainly "evaporate."

I would by no means insinuate that all young women use slang as coarse as this, but I acknowledge to have heard some of these phrases from friends whom I really esteem. Is not the use of these phrases, and of phrases like them whose number is legion, a very vulgar habit? It seems so to me, and I can hear them from the lips of no pretty woman except with pain, and a certain degree of diminution of my respect for her. The habit certainly detracts from womanly dignity. It can be dropped without the slightest danger of going into that extreme of precision in the use of language, which takes out all the life and freedom from social intercourse. Slang is bad enough in young men, and they indulge in far too much of it; but in a young woman, it is disgusting. It is not the outgrowth of fine natures; it is not accordant with refined taste. Any young woman who indulges in it does it at a very sad expense to her mind, and manners, and reputation. Therefore, beware of it; discard it; guard the door of your lips, and leave it to those coarse specimens of your sex of whose natures and habits of thought it is the natural and fitting expression.

One more bad habit of your tongues, and I conclude. It is very common for young women to imagine that all tradesmen have a desire to cheat them. They will talk to the provision dealers and peddlers who call at their doors, and to tradesmen in their shops, with a harshness that would not be forgiven in a man. Men become hardened to this kind of thing, and expect it; and very naturally choose those who suspect them, and accuse them of cheating—who chaffer, and cheapen, and find fault—for the victims of their sharpest operations. A young woman who treats every man with whom she trades as a gentleman, giving him her confidence, and throwing herself upon his honor and generosity, will stand the best possible chance to be fairly dealt by. I except Jews with China ware, and men of Celtic origin with short pipes in their mouths. It is always safe to close a bargain with such persons before entering into any operations; but even this may be done without loss of self-respect. If you see that a man designs to cheat you, it is not lady-like to put yourself upon a footing with him, and undertake to extort a bargain from him. Dismiss him without a word. You cannot afford to waste any breath or self-respect upon him.

Because a man has a thing to sell—because he stands behind a counter, or drives a cart, he is not necessarily no gentleman. As a general thing, those men deserve just as considerate politeness at your hands as if they were in your parlor. You have no right to banter them. You have no right to suspect them— to say harsh things to them—to depreciate their wares, and to place them practically in the position of sharpers and knaves. It is not lady-like for you to put their politeness to the test. They will not insult you, and in that very fact vindicate their claim to your good opinion and polite treatment. You may get the credit with them of being sharp, hard customers, but they will dislike you, and if they speak of you, will not say anything to flatter you.

LETTER VII.

HOUSEWIFERY AND INDUSTRY.

She layeth her hands to the spindle, and her hands hold the distaff. * * She is not afraid of the snow for her household; for all her household are clothed with scarlet. * * * Strength and honor are her clothing, and she shall rejoice in time to come.

SOLOMON.

AMONG the more homely but most essential accomplishments of a young woman is that of housewifery. There are many things at the present day to interfere with its acquisition, but the fact that it is essential should lead you to subordinate to it those which are not. We hear a great deal about the laziness of the present generation of girls. I think the accusation is unjust. Girls who acquire a really good education now, accomplish much more genuine hard work than those in "the good old times" who only learned to read and write, and occupied the most of their time in the kitchen and dairy. Nothing that can be called education and accomplishment can be achieved without great labor and, in my opinion, the principal reason why good housewifery is so much neglected, as an accomplishment, is, that the time is so much occupied in study. Laziness is very apt to come with wealth, and there are undoubtedly a great many more lazy girls now than fifty years ago. They are certainly a very undesirable article to have about, and I pity the poor fellow who gets one of them for a companion; but I say candidly that I do not think there are any more naturally lazy girls in the world than usual.

You expect, one of these days, to be the mistress of a house. Your comfort and happiness, and the comfort and happiness of your husband, will depend very much upon your ability to order that house well. If your companion be in humble circumstances, you will very likely be obliged to do the most of your work yourself. In this case, a thorough knowledge of, and taste for housewifery will be very necessary to you. If you marry a man of competence or wealth, a knowledge of good housewifery is quite as essential to you as if you were required to do your own work. The expenses of your house will be large or small, as you are a bad or a good housekeeper. If you do not know how to do the work of the house; if you have no practical knowledge of all the offices and economies of an establishment, you will be dependent. So far from being the mistress of your house, you will be only its guest. Your servants will circumvent you, they will cheat you, they will make you miserable. If they do not perform their work properly, through wilfulness or ignorance, you cannot tell them better. You will scold them for things which you cannot tell them how to mend, you will be unjust, and you will not keep them. Many a really good servant is constantly suffering from grievances growing directly from the ignorance of her mistress. Unless you are willing to take up for life with a boarding-house—a place for people to vegetate in—you must be a good housewife. It matters not whether you are rich or poor. You need a practical knowledge of cookery, of the laundry, of the prices and qualities of provisions, of chamber work—of everything that enters into the details of home life.

Of course, if you have no mother who is capable of teaching you these things, you are in a measure excusable for not learning them. I pity a family of girls whose mother is a know-nothing and a do-nothing. I do not blame girls for not wishing to put themselves under the tuition of the cook and the maid-of-all-work. But even when you find yourselves under disadvantages like these, you cannot afford to become a woman without knowing something of the homely utilities of life. Your own aptness of mind—your own good sense and ready ingenuity—will give you a clue to the mysteries which practice will ultimately make plain. Your comfort, your independence, your reputation, your husband's respect for you, depend so much upon your ability to keep house well, that I cannot leave the subject without insisting upon the importance of your learning to do it while you have the chance. There are few higher compliments that can be paid to a young woman than that which accords to her the character of an excellent housekeeper. There is no reputation which will more thoroughly tend to confirm a young woman in the esteem of young men, or more forcibly commend her to their esteem than that of being acquainted, practically, with the details of the kitchen and the economies of housekeeping.

This naturally introduces me to a discussion of the benefits of physical industry, and the assumption of regular household duties. There is no better relief to study than the regular performance of special duties in the house. To feel that one is really doing something every day, that the house is the tidier for one's efforts, and the comfort of the family enhanced, is the surest warrant of content and cheerfulness. There is something about this habit of daily work—this regular performance of duty—which tends to regulate the passions, to give calmness and vigor to the mind, to impart healthy tone to the body, and to diminish the desire fo. life in the street and for resort to gossiping companions.

Were I as rich as Crœsus, my girls should have something to do regularly, just as soon as they should become old enough to do anything. They should, in the first place, make their own bed, and take care of their own room. They should dress each other. They should sweep a portion of the house. They should learn, above all things, to help themselves, and thus to be independent in all circumstances. A woman, helpless from any other cause than sickness, is essentially a nuisance. There is nothing womanly and ladylike in helplessness. My policy would be, as girls grow up, to assign to them special duties, first in one part of the house, then in another, until they should become acquainted with all housewifely offices; and I should have an object in this beyond the simple acquisition of a knowledge of house wifery. It should be for the acquisition of habits of physical industry—of habits that conduce to the health of body and mind—of habits that give them an insight into the nature of labor, and inspire within them a genuine sympathy with those whose lot it is to labor.

All young mind is uneasy if it be good for anything. There is not the genuine human stuff in a girl who is habitually and by nature passive, placid, and inactive. The body and the mind must both be in motion. If this tendency to activity be left to run loose—undirected into channels of usefulness—a spoiled child is the result. A girl growing up to womanhood, is, when unemployed, habitually uneasy. The mind aches and chafes because it wants action, for a motive. Now a mind in this condition is not benefited by the command to stay at home, or the withdrawal from companions. It must be set to work. This vital energy that is struggling to find relief in demonstration should be so directed that habits may be formed,—habits of industry that obviate the wish for change and unnecessary play, and form a regular drain upon it. Otherwise, the mind becomes dissipated, the will irresolute, and confinement irksome. Girls will never be happy, except in the company of their playmates, unless home becomes to them a scene of regular duty and personal usefulness.

There is another obvious advantage to be derived from the habit of engaging daily upon special household duties. The imagination of girls is apt to become active to an unhealthy degree, when no corrective is employed. False views of life are engendered, and labor is regarded as menial. Ease comes to be looked upon as a supremely desirable thing, so that when the real, inevitable cares of life come, there is no preparation for them, and weak complainings or ill-natured discontent are the result.

And here I am naturally introduced to another subject. Young women, the glory of your life is to do something and to be something. You very possibly may have formed the idea that ease and personal enjoyment are the ends of your life. This is a terrible mistake. Development in the broadest sense and in the highest direction is the end of your life. You may possibly find ease with it, and a great deal of precious personal enjoyment, or your life may be one long experience of self-denial. If you wish to be something more than the pet and plaything of a man; if you would rise above the position of a pretty toy, or the ornamental fixture of an establishment, you have got a work to do. You have got a position to maintain in society; you have got the poor and the sick to visit; you may possibly have a family to rear and train; you have got to take a load of care upon your shoulders and bear it through life. You have got a character to sustain; and I hope that you will have the heart of a husband to cheer and strengthen. Ease is not for you. Selfish enjoyment is not for you. The world is to be made better by you. You have got to suffer and to work; and if there be a spark of the true fire in you, your hearts will respond to these words.

The time will come when you shall see that all your toil, and care, and pain, and sorrow, and practical sympathy for others has built you up into a strength of womanhood which will despise ease as an end of life, and pity those who are content with it. Get this idea that your great business is simply to live at ease out of your head at once. There is nothing noble and ennobling in it. Your mental and physical powers can only give you worthy happiness in the using. They were made for use; and a lazy woman is inevitably miserable. I do not put this matter of enjoyment before you as the motive for action. I simply state the fact that it is a result of action—an incident of a life worthily spent.

When you have properly comprehended and received this idea, the recreations of life and the pleasures of social intercourse will take their appropriate positions with relation to the business of life—its staple duties. Recreation will become re-creation—simply the renewal of your powers, that they may all the better perform the work which you have undertaken, or which circumstances have devolved upon you. Social pleasure will rise into a sympathetic communion with natures and lives earnest like your own, upon the subjects nearest your hearts, and it will give you strength and guidance.

The pleasures of life will become the wells,scattered along the way, where you will lay down your burdens for the moment, wipe your brows, and drink, that you may go into the work before you refreshed in body and mind. In these quiet hours you will feel a healthy thrill of happiness which those who seek pleasure for its own sake never know.

There are few objects in this world more repulsive to me than a selfish woman—a woman who selfishly consults her own enjoyments, her own ease, her own pleasure. If you have the slightest desire to be loved; if you would have your presence a welcome one in palace and cottage alike; if you would be admired, respected, revered; if you would have all sweet human sympathies clustering around you while you live, and the tears of a multitude of friends shed upon your grave when you die, you must be a working woman—living and working for others, denying yourself for others, and building up for yourself a character, strong symmetrical, beautiful. If I were you, I would rather be that insensate and quietly gliding shadow which the wounded soldier kissed as the noble Florence Nightingale passed his weary pillow, than the pampered creature of luxury, who has no thought above her personal ease and personal adornment.

Do not seek out for yourselves any prominent field

of service where you will attract the attention of the world. Remain where God places you. Some of the noblest heroisms of the world have been achieved in humble life. The poor ye have always with you. The miserable are always around you. You can lighten your father's burdens. You can restrain your brothers from vicious society. You can relieve your failing and fading mother of much care. You can gather the ragged and ignorant children at your knee, and teach them something of a better life than they have seen. You can become angels of light and goodness to many stricken hearts. You can read to the aged. You can do many things which will be changed to blessings upon your own soul. Florence Nightingale did her work in her place; do your work in yours, and your Father who seeth in secret shall reward you openly.

I would be the last one to cast a shadow on your brows, but I would undeceive you at the first, so that you may begin life with right ideas. Life is real—it is a real and earnest thing. It has homely details, painful passages, and a crown of care for every brow. I seek to inspire you with a wish and a will to meet it with a womanly spirit. I seek to point you to its nobler meanings and its higher results. The tinsel with which your imagination has invested it will all fall off of itself, so soon as you shall fairly enter upon its experiences.

Then if these ideas have no place in you, you will be obliged to acquire them slowly and painfully, or you will sink into a poor, selfish, discontented creature—and be, so far as others are concerned, either a nonentity, or a disagreeable hanger-on and looker-on. So I say, begin to take up life's duties now. Learn something of what life is, before you take upon yourself its graver responsibilities.

LETTER VIII.

THE BEAUTY AND BLESSEDNESS OF FEMALE PIETY.

The cross, if rightly borne, shall be
No burden, but support to thee.

WHITTIER.

YOUNG women, this is my last letter addressed specially to you; and as I take your hand, and give you my adieu, I wish to say a few words which shall be worth a great deal to you. It is my opinion that to a certain extent, in certain directions, God meant that you should be dependent upon men, and that in this dependence should exist some of your profoundest and sweetest attractions and your noblest characteristics. Your bodies are smaller than those of men. You were not made to wrestle with the rough forces of nature. You were not made for war, nor commerce, nor agriculture.

In all these departments, the iron wills and the iron muscles of man are alone at home. The bread you eat, and the fabrics you wear, are to be gathered from the earth by men. You are to be protected by men. They build your houses; they guard your persons. It is entirely natural for you to rely upon them for much that you have. You give, or may give, great rewards for all this. It is not a menial relation, nor one which detracts from your dignity in the least. The circle of human duties is only complete by the union of those of man and woman. Man has his sphere—woman, hers. We cannot talk of superiority among spheres and duties that are alike essential. Suffice it that, in the degree in which you are dependent upon man for support and protection, does he owe support and protection to you. He is bound to do for you what you, through the peculiarities of your constitution, are unable to do for yourself. You are never to quarrel with this arrangement. You will only make yourself unhappy by it, because, by quarrelling with God's plans, you essentially unsex yourself, and become a discord. Therefore, recognise your dependence gladly and gracefully. Be at home in it for in it lies your power for influence and for good.

This advances us a step towards the point to which I wish to lead you. Now, if you will go with me into a circle of praying Christians, or if you will take up with me a list of the members of any church, I will show you a fact which I wish to connect with the facts stated in the preceding paragraph. You will find, I suppose, that at least two-thirds of the members of the prayer-meeting are women, and that the church register will show a corresponding proportion of female names. Why is this? Is it because women are weaker than men, simply? Is it because women are subject to smaller temptations than men? Is it because their passions are less powerful than those of men? Not at all—or not in any important degree. It is because a feeling of dependence is native in the female heart. It is because the pride of independence has little or no place there. It is because the female mind has to undergo comparatively a small revolution to become religious. Rather, perhaps, I should say, that one powerful barrier that stands before the path of every man in his approach to the valley of humiliation does not oppose the passage of the true woman. I suppose it is very rare that those who are denominated "strong-minded women" become religious. The pride of personal independence is built before them by their own hands.

So sweet and so natural a thing is piety among women that men have come to regard a woman without it as strange, if not unhealthy. The coarsest and most godless men often select pious wives, because they see that piety softens, and deepens, and elevates every natural grace of person, and every accomplishment of mind. Now my opinion is that Heaven, seeing how important it is for you to be its own children, in profession and in spirit, has given special favors to your sex, through this simple fact or principle of dependence. It is your work to soften and refine men. Men living without you, by themselves, become savage and sinful. The purer you are, the more are they restrained, and the more are they elevated. It is your work to form the young mind,—to give it direction and instruction—to develop its love for the good and the true. It is your work to make home happy—to nourish all the virtues, and instil all the sentiments which build men up into good citizens. The foundation of our national character is laid by the mothers of the nation. I say that Heaven, seeing the importance to the world of piety in you, has so modified your relations to man that it shall be comparatively easy for you to descend into that valley, over which all must walk, before their feet can stand upon the heights of Christian experience, between which and Heaven's door the ascent is easy.

For my own part, I shrink with horror from a godless woman. There seems to be no light in her—no glory proceeding from her. There is something monstrous about her. I can see why men do not become religious. It is a hard thing—it is, at least, if experience and observation are to be relied on—for a man whose will has been made stern by encounters in the great battle of life, who is conscious of power and accustomed to have the minds around him bend to his, who possesses the pride of manhood and the self-esteem that springs naturally in the mind of one in his position, to become "as a little child." Woman has only to recognise her dependence upon One higher than man, and, in doing this, is obliged to do but little violence to her habits of thought, and no violence at all to such sentiments of independence as stand most in the way of man. So I say that a godless woman is a monstrous woman. She is an unreasonable woman. She is an offensive woman. Even an utterly godless man, unless he be debauched and debased to the position of an animal, deems such a woman without excuse. He looks on her with suspicion. He would not have such an one to take the care of his children. He would not trust her.

I do not propose to offer you any incentives to piety drawn from a future condition of rewards and punishments. I leave it to the pulpits whose ministrations you attend to talk of this matter in their own way. My whole argument shall relate to the proprieties and necessities of the present life. It is proper that you serve the Being who made you, and that you love the One who redeemed you. It is proper that to all your graces you add that of unselfishness. It is proper that all the elements of your character be harmonized and sublimated by the tenderest devotion to the "One altogether lovely." It is proper that your heart be purified, so that all the influence which goes out of it, through the varied relationships of life, be good, and only good. I mean by the word "proper" all that the word proper can mean. It is eternally and immutably fit. I mean that it is *improper* and *unfit* that you should fail of piety. I mean that by carrying with you a rebellious and cold and careless heart, you introduce among the sweet harmonies of the world, a harsh discord, which it is not fit and proper that you should introduce. You are a wandering star. You are a voiceless bird. You are a motionless brook. The strings of your soul are not in tune with those chords which the Infinite hand sweeps as he evolves the music of the universe. Your being does not respond to the touch of Providence; and if Beauty, and Truth, and Goodness, and Love, come down to you, like angels out of heaven, and sing you their sweetest songs, you do not see their wings, nor recognise their home and parentage. I say that it is not proper—it is inexpressibly unfit that you—a woman—with delicate sensibilities, and pure instincts and a dependent nature, should ignore the relations which exist between your soul and God, and put a veil of blackness between the light which he has lighted within you, and that Infinite fountain of ight still open and ready to fill all your being with its divine radiance.

Then, as to your necessities: First, remember what you are. You are really the consolers of the world. You attend the world in sickness; you give all its medicines; your society soothes the world after its toil, and rewards it for its perplexities; you receive the infant when it enters upon existence; you drape the cold form of the aged when life is past; you settle the little difficulties, and assuage the sorrows of childhood; you minister to the poor and the distressed. Do you suppose that out of the resources of your poor heart, you can supply all the draughts that will be made upon your sympathies and their varied ministry? Do you believe that you carry within your own bosom light for the dying, hope for the despairing, consolation for the bereft, patience for the sick? Nay, do you believe that you have light and hope and consolation and patience sufficient for your own soul's wants, while performing the ministries to which, in Heaven's economy, you are appointed? Piety is, then, an absolute necessity to you. You can no more perform these offices to which you are called, properly and efficiently, without piety, than a bird can fly without wings. You would be trying to make bricks without straw. Think of a woman by the side of a dying sister, or a sick child, or a sorrowing friend, or a broken-hearted and broken-spirited man, without a word of heaven in her mouth—without so much as the ability to whisper "Our Father," or even to point her finger hopefully towards the stars!

Again, your life and duties are peculiar, as your sphere is distinct. If you lead a worthy, womanly life, it will be a home life—free from great excitements. The current of your thoughts will flow in retired channels. You will hear, outside, the braying of trumpets, and the roll of drums, and the din of wheels, and the rush and roar of the world's great business. Oftentimes, when you are busy with your modest affairs, and going through the wearying routine of your life, you will be tempted to repine at their quietness and insipidness. Many a woman does the work of her life without being seen or noticed by the world. The world sees a family reared to virtue—one child after another growing into Christian manhood and womanhood, and at last it sees them all gathered around a grave where the mother that bore them rests from her labors. But the world has never seen that quiet woman laboring for her children, making their clothes, providing their food, teaching them their prayers, and making their homes comfortable and happy.

The world knows nothing, or does not think, of the fears, the pains, and the anxieties inseparable from the mother's office. She bears them alone, and discharges her peculiar responsibilities without assistance. No individual in the world can do a mother's work for her A family of young immortals is committed to her hands. The rearing and training of these form a business to which she has served no apprenticeship. If divine guidance and support be necessary to any one in the world, they are necessary to the wife and mother. It is a sad, sad thought to any son or daughter that his or her mother was not a woman of piety. The boy that feels that his name is mentioned in a good mother's prayers, is comparatively safe from vice, and the ruin to which it leads. The sweetest thought that N. P. Willis ever penned grew out of a reference to his pious mother's prayers for him. Tossed by the waves, in a vessel which was bearing him homeward, he wrote:

"Sleep safe, O wave-worn mariner,
Nor fear to-night nor storm nor sea!
The ear of Heaven bends low to her;
He comes to shore who sails with me!"

Will not piety be necessary to you? Will not your piety be necessary to your children?

And now, young women, a few closing words. I have no doubt many of you have read these letters with care, and with an earnest wish to profit by them. They have been written in all honesty and sincerity, and I leave them with you. The opinions I have given you have not been hastily formed, nor has the counsel I have urged upon you arisen from anything but a conscientious conviction of your wants, and a desire to help you to a womanhood, the noblest to be achieved in this world. Your happiness is very much in your own hands; so are your usefulness and your good name. I do not ask you to be anything but a glad, sunny woman. I would have no counsels of mine recommended by long faces and formal behavior. I would have you so at peace with Heaven, with the world and with yourself, that tears shall flow only at the call of sympathy. I would have you immaculate as light, devoted to all good deeds, industrious, intelligent, patient, heroic. And crowning every grace of person and mind, every accomplishment, every noble sentiment, every womanly faculty, every delicate instinct, every true impulse, I would see religion upon your brow—the coronet by token of which God makes you a princess in his family, and an heir to the brightest glories, the sweetest pleasures, the noblest privileges, and the highest honors of his kingdom.

Letters to Young Married People.

LETTERS TO YOUNG MARRIED PEOPLE.

---o---

LETTER I.

THE FIRST ESSENTIAL DUTIES OF THE CONNUBIAL RELATION

> O let us walk the world, so that our love
> Burn like a blessed beacon, beautiful,
> Upon the walls of life's surrounding dark!
>
> GERALD MASSEY.

YOU are married, and it is for better or for worse. You are bound to one another as companions for life. Did it ever occur to you that this is a stupendous, a momentous fact? Did you ever think that since you ame into the world, a precious lump of helpless life, there is no fact of your history which will so much affect your destiny as this? I do not propose to inquire into the motives which led you to this union. You may have come together like two streams, flowing naturally towards one point, and then mingling their waters with scarcely a ripple, to pass on together to the great ocean. You may have come together under the wild stress of passion, or the feeble attractions of fancy, or the sordid compulsions of interest, or by force of a love so pure that an angel would think himself in heaven while in its presence. But the time for considering the motives which have united you is past. You are married, for better or for worse. The word is spoken. The bond is sealed; and the only question now is—"how shall this union be made to contribute the most to your happiness and your best development?" It is to answer this question as well as I can, that I write this series of letters.

You have but one life to live, and no amount of money, or influence, or fame, can pay you for a life of unhappiness. You cannot afford to be unhappy. You cannot afford to quarrel with one another. You cannot afford to cherish a single thought, to harbor a single desire, to gratify a single passion, nor indulge a single selfish feeling that will tend to make this union anything but a source of happiness to you. So it becomes you, at starting, to have a perfect understanding with one another. It becomes you to resolve that you will be happy together, at any rate; or that if you suffer, it shall be from the same cause, and in perfect sympathy. You are not to let any human being step between you, under any circumstances. Neither father nor mother, neither brother nor sister, neither friend nor neighbor, has any right to interfere with your relations, so long, at least, as you are agreed. You twain are to be one flesh—identified in objects, desires, sympathies, fortunes, positions—everything. You are to know no closer friend. Now I care not how pure and genuine may be the love which has brought you together, if you have any character at all, you will find that this perfect union cannot be effected without compromises. Human character, by a wise provision of Providence, is infinitely varied, and there are not two individuals in existence so entirely alike in their tastes, habits of thought, and natural aptitudes, that they can keep step with one another over all the rough places in the path of life. So there must be a bending to one another. I suppose the brides are few who have not wept once over the hasty words of a husband not six months married; and I suppose there are few husbands who, in the early part of their married life, have not felt that perhaps their choice was not a wise one.

Breaches of harmony will occur between imperfect men and women; but all bad results may be avoided by a resolution, well kept on both sides, to ask the other's pardon for every offence—for the hasty word. the peevish complaint, the unshared pleasure—everything that awakens an unpleasant thought, or wounds a sensibility. This reparation must be made at once and if you have a frank and worthy nature, a quarrel is impossible. My opinion is that ninety-nine one-hundredths of the unhappiness in the connubial relation, is the absolute fault, and not primarily the misfortune, of the parties. You can be happy together if you will; but the agreement to be happy must be mutual. The compromise cannot be all on one side. It is a mulish pride in men, and a sensitive will in women, that make the principal difficulty in all unhappy cases. I say to every man and woman, if you have done anything which has displeased your companion, beg her or his pardon, whether you were intentionally guilty or not. It is the cheapest and quickest way to settle the business. One confession makes way for another, and the matter is closed—closed, most probably, with the very sweetest kiss of the season.

Be frank with one another. Many a husband and wife go on from year to year with thoughts in their hearts, that they hesitate to reveal to one another. If you have anything in your mind concerning your companion that troubles you, out with it. Do not brood over it. Perhaps it can be explained on the spot, and the matter for ever put to rest. Draw your souls closer and closer together, from year to year. Get all obstacles out of the way. Just as soon as one arises, attend to it, and get rid of it. At last, they will all disappear. You will become wonted to one another's habits and frames of mind and peculiarities of disposition; and love, respect, and charity will take care of the rest.

I insist on this, because it is the very first essential thing. I insist on it, because I believe that if there be sufficient affinity between two persons to bring them together, and to lead them to unite their lives, it is their fault if they fail to live happily, and still more and more happily as the years advance. I will go so far as to say that I believe there are few women with whom a kind, sensible man may not live happily, if he be so disposed; and I know that woman is more plastic in her nature, and more susceptible to love than man. So, when I hear of unhappy matches, I know that somebody is to blame.

This intimate association of husband and wife—nay, this identity—can never be preserved while either is blabbing of the other. A man who tells his neighbors that his wife is extravagant, that she is wasteful, that he never finds her home, that she will never go out with him, or that she is or does anything which he desires her not to be or do, does a shameful thing, and a cruel thing, besides making a fool of himself. A woman whc bruits her husband's faults, who tells the neighbors how much he seeks the society of other women, how much he spends for cigars, how late he is out at night, how lazy he is, how little he cares for what interests her, how stingy he is with his money, and all that sort of thing, sins against herself, and consents, or voluntarily enlists, to publish that which is essentially her own shame. A husband and wife have no business to tell one another's faults to anybody but to one another. They cannot do it without shame. Their grievances are to be settled in private, between themselves; and in all public places, and among friends, they are to preserve towards one another that nice consideration and entire respectfulness which their relation enjoins. For they are one in the law; and for a man or woman to publish the truth, that they are not one in fact, is to acknowledge that they are living in the relation of an unwilling lover and a compulsory mistress.

A great deal of evil might be prevented between you if you would allow your affection to give itself natural expression. I know of husbands so proud and stiff and surly that they never have a kiss or a caress, or a fond word for their wives whom they really love. I know such husbands who have most lovable wives—wives to whom a single tender demonstration, that shall tell to their hearts how inexpressibly pleasant their faces and their society are, and how fondly they are loved, would be better than untold gold—wives, to whom caresses are sweeter than manna, and fond words more musical than robin-songs in the rain. They go through life starving for them—bearing buds of happiness upon their bosoms that must be kissed into bloom, or wither and fall. Yet the cast-iron husband goes about his business without even a courteous "good morning," eats his meals with immense regularity, provides for his family exemplarily, imagines that he is an excellent husband, and entertains a profound contempt for silly people who are fond of one another.

Heaven be thanked that there are some in the world to whose hearts the barnacles will not cling! Heaven be thanked for the young old boys and the young old girls—boys and girls for ever—who, until the evening of life falls upon them, interchange the sweet caresses that call back the days of courtship and early marriage! Thank Heaven that my wife can never grow old; that so long as a lock adorns her temples, brown or grey, my finger shall toy with it; that so long as I can sit there shall be a place for her on my knee; and that so long as I can whisper and she can hear, she shall know by fond confession that her soul is next to mine—linked to mine—mine!

I wish in this letter to impress upon you the idea which few married people apparently thoroughly comprehend, that you—husband and wife—are one,—that you have no separate interests, that you can have no separate positions in society, that you should desire none, and that it is within your ability, and is most imperatively your duty to be happy together. In order to be what you should be to each other, and in order to be happy yourselves—in your own hearts—you should begin right. You should be willing at all times to bear one another's burdens; and in fact, I know of no better rule for accomplishing the end I seek for you than by your constantly studying and ministering to the happiness of each other. Selfishness is the bane of all life, and especially of married life; and if a husband and wife devote themselves to one another's happiness, relinquishing their own selfish gratification for that end, the task is accomplished—the secret solved. The path of such a pair is paved with gold. Their life is a song of praise. All good angels are about them, bearing consolations for every sorrow, antidotes for every bane, rewards for every labor, and strength for every trial. That is essential marriage; and, as Paul Dombey said when Mrs. Pipchin told him there was nobody else like her, "that is a very good thing."

I suppose there is a modicum of romance in most natures, and that if it gather about any event, it is that of marriage. Most people marry ideals. There is more or less of fictitious and fallacious glory resting upon the head of every bride, which the inchoate husband sees and believes in. Both men and women manufacture perfections in their mates by a happy process of their imaginations, and then marry them. This, of course, wears away. By the time the husband has seen his wife eat heartily of pork and beans, and, with her hair frizzled, and her oldest dress on, full of the enterprise of overhauling things, he sees that she belongs to the same race with himself. And she, when her husband gets up cross in the morning, and undertakes to shave himself with cold water and a dull razor, while his suspenders dangle at his heels, begins to see that man is a very prosaic animal. In other words, there is such a thing as a honeymoon, of longer or shorter duration; and while the moonshine lasts, the radiance of the seventh heaven cannot compare with it. It is a very delicious little delirium—a febrile mental disease—which, like measles, never comes again.

When the honeymoon passes away, setting behind dull mountains, or dipping silently into the stormy sea of life, the trying hour of married life has come. Between the parties, there are no more illusions. The feverish desire of possession has gone—vanished into gratification—and all excitement has receded. Then begins, or should begin, seriously, the business of adaptation. If they find that they do not love one another as they thought they did, they should conscientiously and earnestly foster and strengthen every bond of attachment which exists. They should double their assiduous attentions to one another, and be jealous of everything which tends in the slightest degree to separate them. Life is too precious to be thrown away in secret regrets or open differences.

I say to any married pair, from whom the romance of life has fled, and who are discontented in the slightest degree with their condition and relations, begin this work of reconciliation before you are a day older. Renew the attentions of earlier days. Draw your hearts closer together. Talk the thing all over. Acknowledge your faults to one another, and determine that henceforth you will be all in all to each other; and, my word for it, you shall find in your relation the sweetest joy earth has for you. There is no other way for you to do. If you are unhappy at home, you must be unhappy abroad. The man or woman who has settled down upon the conviction that he or she is attached for life to an uncongenial yoke-fellow, and that there is no way of escape, has lost life. There is no effort too costly to be made which can restore to its setting upon their bosoms the missing pearl.

LETTER II.

SPECIAL DUTIES OF THE HUSBAND.

He that loveth his wife loveth himself. For no man ever yet hated his own flesh; but nourisheth and cherisheth it, even as the Lord the church.

St. Paul.

YOUNG husband, this letter is for you. Have you an idea that you have anything like a just comprehension of the nature of the being whom God has given you for a companion? If you have, you labor under a very serious mistake. You may live with her until, amid grey hairs and grandchildren, you celebrate your golden wedding, and then know but a tithe of her strength and tenderness. I believe in such a thing as sex of soul. A woman's happiness flows to her from sources and through channels, different from those which give origin and conduct to the happiness of man, and,

8*

in a measure, will continue to do so for ever. Her faculties bend their exercise towards different issues; her social and spiritual natures demand a different aliment. What will satisfy you will not satisfy her. That which most interests you is not that in which her soul finds its most grateful exercise. Her love for you may bring her intimately into sympathy with your pursuits, through all their wide range, from a hotly driven political contest to breaking up a piece of wild land, or even to the cultivation of an unthrifty whisker; but it will only be because they interest the man she loves above all others. She is actuated by motives that do not affect you at all, or not to the extent that they do her If she be led into sin, you renounce and denounce her as a thing unclean; yet, through all your debauchery, your untruth to her, your beastly drunkenness, your dishonor, your misfortune, she will cling to you. There is in her heart a depth of tenderness of which neither you nor she herself has any conception. Only the circumstances and exigencies of life will reveal it; and this is why a healthy female soul is always fresh and new. Longfellow, in his "Spanish Student," gives a hint of this—and a pretty deep one—in the language he puts into the mouth of Preciosa's lover:—

> "What most I prize in woman
> Is her affections, not her intellect.

The intellect is finite; but the affections
Are infinite, and cannot be exhausted."

* * * * * * * *

'The world of the affections is thy world;—
Not that of man's ambition. In that stillness,
Which most becomes a woman, calm and holy,
Thou sittest by the fireside of the heart,
Feeding its flame."

"The affections are infinite, and cannot be exhausted;" and it is through her affections, and through the deepest of all affections, that happiness comes to the bosom of your wife. The world may pile its honors upon you until your brain goes wild with delirious excitement; wealth may pour into your coffers through long years of prosperity; you may enjoy the fairest rewards of enterprise and excellence; but if all these things are won by depriving your wife of your society —by driving her out of your thoughts, and by interfering with the constant sympathetic communion of your heart with hers, she cannot but feel that what enriches you impoverishes her, and that your gain, whatever it may be, is at her expense. She may enjoy your reputation and your wealth, your successes and good fortunes, but you and your society are things that are infinitely more precious to her. She depends upon you, naturally and by force of circumstances. Friends may crowd around her; but if you come not, she is not satisfied. She may have spread before her a thousand delicacies ; but if they are unshared with you, she would exchange them all for an orange which you bring home to her as an evidence that you have thought of her The dress you selected when in the city is the dearest, though she may acknowledge to herself that she would have chosen different colors and material. In short, it is from your heart, and the world coming through your heart, that she draws that sustenance and support which her deepest nature craves.

Now, how are you dealing by this wife of yours? Do you say that you have all you can attend to in your business, and that she must look out for herself? Do you forget that she lives in the house, away from the excitements of the world which so much interest you, and that the very sweetest excitement of the day is that which throws the warm blood in her heart into eddies as she hears your step at the door? Do you forget that she has no pleasure in public places unless you are at her side? Are you unmindful that she has no such pleasant walks as those which she takes with her hand upon your arm? Do you ignore the fact that she has a claim upon your time? Do you fail to remember that you took her out of a pleasant family circle, away from the associations of her childhood, and that she has no society in all the wide world which she prizes so highly as yours? Do you forget that you owe your first duty to her, and that you have no right to give to society, or to your own pleasure, the time which necessarily involves neglect of her? To come to a practical point—is it one of the aims of your life to give to your wife a portion of your time and society, so that she shall not always be obliged to sit alone, and go out alone?

There are some poor specimens of your sex in the world who not only do not feel that their wives have any special claim on their consideration and their time, but who take the occasion, when in the presence of their wives, to make themselves generally despicable. I know a man whose appearance when in society, or mingling in the common affairs of business, has all the blandness and fragrance of newly mown hay. He touches his hat to the ladies whom he meets in the street with a grace which a D'Orsay would honor with admiration, and gives them a smile as genial and radiant as a harvest moon. He bears with him all the polish and grace of a gentleman. The concentrated virtues of all the lubricating oils could not add to the ease of his manners. People cannot imagine how such a man could be anything but the best of husbands; but he is not any such thing. If I were a Jew, and not particularly fond of bacon, I should say that he was a hog in his own house. He is, there, domineering, peevish, exacting, and hateful. I have never known him to speak an affectionate or pleasant word to the best of wives. Nothing is out of place in the house for which she is not reproached in fretful and insulting language Nothing goes wrong out of doors for which he does no take revenge, or show his spite, by finding fault with the companion of his life. He criticises her cooking and her personal appearance, and, in short, lets off upon her wounded but patient ear all the foul accumulations of his miserable nature and most contemptible disposition. Although some powerful impressions received in early life have induced me to oppose corporeal punishment on principle, I have sometimes wondered whether I should be entirely inconsolable if he should, some time, be cowhided, kicked, cuffed, maimed, and otherwise shamefully entreated.

But this is an extreme case, you say. Well, it ought to be; but will you just stop for a moment, and ask yourself where it is that you show the worst side of your nature? Where is it that you feel at the greatest liberty to exhibit your spleen, to give way to your fretfulness, to speak harsh words, to make hateful little speeches that are contemptible from their unprovoked bitterness? Is it among your fellows, and in the society of other ladies, that you take occasion to say your meanest things? No, sir! You go home to your wife;

you go home from those who care no more for you than they do for a thousand others, to the woman whom in the presence of God and men you have promised to love and cherish above all others; to the woman who loves you, and who regards you as better than all else earthly; to a woman who is unprotected save by you, and wholly unprotected from you, and spit your spleen into her ear, and say things to her which, if any one else were to say, would secure him a well deserved caning. Are you not ashamed of this? You say things to her which you would not dare to say to any other lady, however much you might be provoked. You say them—O courageous friend! because nobody has the right to cowhide you for it. Isn't that brave and manly? As the good mothers of us all have told us a thousand times, "don't you never let me hear of your doing that again." It isn't pretty. It is ineffably wicked and dastardly.

That husbands and wives may entertain perfect sympathy, there should be the closest confidence between them. I need not tell the wife to give her husband the most perfect confidence in all affairs. She does this naturally, if her husband do not repulse her. But you, young husband, do not give your wife your confidence—you do not make her your confidante—you have an idea that your business is not your wife's business. So you keep your troubles, your successes—everything—to yourself. Numberless disturbances of married life begin exactly at this point. Your wife receives the money for her personal expenses, and for the expenses of the house, at your hands. You do not tell her how hardly it has been won; with how much difficulty you have contrived to get it into your purse, and how necessary it is for her to be economical. You often deceive her, out of genuine love for her, into the belief that you are really doing very well; and yet you wonder the woman can give ten dollars for a hat and thirty dollars for a cloak. Perhaps you chide her for her extravagance, and so, in course of time, she comes to think you have got a niggardly streak in you, and very naturally rebels against it. She will not be curtailed in her expenditures. She dresses no better than her neighbors. So you run your fingers through your hair, and sigh over the fact that you have got an extravagant wife, while she, in turn, wonders how it is possible for a loving husband to be so selfish and stingy

Thus for life, perhaps, a hostility of feeling and nterest is established, which might all have been prevented by a free and full statement of your circumstances. This would interest her in, and identify her with, all your trials. It is entirely rational and right that your wife should understand the basis of all your requirements of her; and, when she does this, the chances are that she will not only be economical herself, but will point out leakages in your prosperity for which you are responsible rather than herself. It is possible that you have a companion as much troubled by figures as the child-wife, Dora, was. If so, I am sorry for you; but, if so, very luckily she will do what you require of her without a reason.

I understand perfectly the desire of a young and sensitive husband to give his wife all the money she wants. You would fulfil her wishes in all things; especially would you allow her those means that will enable her to gratify her tastes in dress and household equipage. You dislike to appear unthrifty, inefficient, or mean, and you are willing to sacrifice much, that no care, no small economies, no apprehension of coming evil, should cloud the brow of the one you love. Well, I honor this feeling, for it has its birth in a sensitive, manly pride; but it may go too far—very much too far. It has carried many a man straight into the open hroat of bankruptcy, and ruined both husband and wife for life. No, you must tell her all about it. She must know what your objects and projects are. She must know what your income is, and the amount of your annual expenses. Then, if she be a good wife, and worthy of a good husband, she will become more thoroughly your partner, and "cut her garment according to the cloth." The interest which you thus secure from her in your business affairs, will be the greatest possible comfort to you. She will enjoy all your successes, for they become her own. She will sympathize in all your trials, and you will find great consolation in feeling that there is one heart in the world that understands you.

And this matter of confidence between you and your wife must be carried into everything, for she is your life partner—your next soul. There is no way by which she can understand fully her relations to the community and its various interests, save by understanding your own. So I say in closing, that to your wife you owe a reasonable portion of your time and society, the very choicest side of your nature and character when in her society, and your fullest confidence in all the affairs connected with your business, your ambitions, your hopes, and your fears. In the fierce conflicts of life you will find abundant recompense for all this. Your wife will soften your resentments, assuage your disappointments, pour balm upon your wounded spirit, and harmonize and soften you. At the same time, the exercise of heart and soul which this will give her, will make her a nobler, freer, better woman. It will give her greater breadth and strength of mind, and deepen her sensibilities. To a pair thus living and acting, may well be applied a couplet which occurs in that charming picture painted by Pinckney, of the Indian husband and his pale-faced wife :—

> "She humanizes him, and he
> Educates her to liberty."

LETTER III.

SPECIAL DUTIES OF THE WIFE.

And when the King's decree which he shall make shall be published throughout all his empire (for it is great), all the wives shall give to their husbands honor, both to great and small.

BOOK OF ESTHER.

Teach the young women to be sober, to love their husbands, to love their children, to be discreet, keepers at home, good, obedient to their own husbands.

ST. PAUL.

YOUNG wife, I talked to your husband in my last letter, and now I address you. I told him that you have a claim on his time and society. There are qualifications of this claim which concern you particularly, and so I speak to you about them. Your husband labors all day—every day—and during the waking hours, between the conclusion of his labor at night and its commencement in the morning, he must have recreation of some kind; and here comes in your duty. If you do not make his home pleasant, so that the fulfilment of his duty to you shall be a sweet pleasure to him, you cannot hope for much of his company. What his nature craves it will have—must have. He cannot be a slave all the time—a slave to his work by day and a slave to you by night. He must have hours of freedom; and happy are you if, of his own choice, he take the enjoyment you offer in the place of anything which the outside world has to give. I suppose there are few men who, when their work is over, and their supper eaten, do not have a desire to go down town "to meet a man," or visit "the post-office." There is a natural desire in every heart to have, every day, an hour of social freedom—a few minutes, at least, of walk in the open air and contact with the minds of other men. This is entirely a natural and necessary thing; and you should encourage rather than seek to prevent it, unless your husband is inclined to visit bad places, and associate with bad companions.

Precisely here is a dangerous point for both husband and wife. The wife has been alone during the day, and thinks that her husband ought to spend the whole evening with her. The husband has been confined to his labor, and longs for an hour of freedom, in whatever direction his feet may choose to wander. Perhaps the wife thinks he has no business to wander at all, and that his custom is to wander too widely and too long. She complains, and becomes exacting. She cannot bear to have her husband out of her sight for a moment, after he quits his work. Now, if there be anything in all this world that will make a husband hate his wife, it is a constant attempt on her part to monopolize all his leisure time and all his society, to curtail his freedom, and a tendency to be for ever fretting his ears with the statement that "she is nothing, of course," that he "does not care anything about her," and that he dislikes his home. Treatment like this will just as certainly rouse all the perverseness in a man's nature as a spark will ignite gunpowder. Injustice and inconsiderateness will not go down, especially when administered by a man's companion. He knows that he loves his home, and that he needs and has a right to a certain amount of his time, away from home; and if he be treated as if he possessed no such necessity and right, he will soon learn to be all that his wife represents him to be. I tell you that a man wants very careful handling. You must remember that he can owe no duty to you which does not involve a duty from you. You have the charge of the home, and if you expect him to spend a portion, or all of his evening in it, you must make it attractive. If you expect a man, as a matter of duty, to give any considerable amount of time to your society, daily, through a long series of years, you are to see that that society is worth something to him. Where are your accomplishments? Where are your books? Where are your subjects of conversation?

But let us take up this question separately: how shall a wife make her home pleasant and her society attractive? This is a short question, but a full answer would make a book. I can only touch a few points. In the first place, she should never indulge in fault-finding. If a man has learned to expect that he will invariably be found fault with by his wife, on his return home, and that the burden of her words will be complaint, he has absolutely no pleasure to anticipate and none to enjoy. There is but one alternative for a husband in such a case: either to steel himself against complaints, or be harrowed up by them and made snappish and waspish. They never produce a good effect, under any circumstances whatever. There should always be a pleasant word and look ready for him who returns from the toils of the day, wearied with earning the necessaries of the family. If a pretty pair of slippers lie before the fire, ready for his feet, so much the better.

Then, again, the desire to be pleasing in person should never leave a wife for a day. The husband who comes home at night, and finds his wife dressed to receive him,

—dressed neatly and tastefully, because she wishes to be pleasant to his eye, cannot, unless he be a brute, neglect her, or slight her graceful pains-taking. It is a compliment to him. It displays a desire to maintain the charms which first attracted him, and to keep intact the silken bonds which her tasteful girlhood had fastened to his fancy.

I have seen things managed very differently from this. I have known an undressed head of "horrid hair" worn all day long, because nobody but the husband would see it. I have seen breakfast dresses with sugar plantations on them of very respectable size, and most disagreeable stickiness. In short, I have seen slatterns, whose kiss would not tempt the hungriest hermit that ever forswore women, and was sorry for it. I have seen them with neither collar nor zone,—with a person which did not possess a single charm to a husband with his eyes open, and in his right mind. This is all wrong, young wife, for there is no being in this world for whom it is so much for your interest to dress, as for your husband. Your happiness depends much on your retaining, not only the esteem of your husband, but his admiration. He should see no greater neatness and no more taste in material and fitness, in any woman's dress, than in yours; and there is no individual in the world before whom you should always appear with more thorough tidiness of person than your husband. If you are careless in this particular, you absolutely throw away some of the strongest and most charming influences which you possess. What is true of your person is also true of your house. If your house be disorderly; if dust cover the table, and invite the critical finger to write your proper title; if the furniture look as if it were tossed into a room from a cart; if your table-cloth have a more intimate acquaintance with gravy than with soap, and from cellar to garret there be no order, do you blame a husband for not wanting to sit down and spend his evening with you? I should blame him, of course on general principles, but, as all men are not so sensible as I am, I should charitably entertain all proper excuses.

Still again, have you anything to talk about—anything better than scandal—with which to interest and refresh his weary mind? I believe in the interchange of caresses, as I have told you before, but kisses are only the spice of life. You cannot always sit on your husband's knee, for, in the first place, it would tire him, and in the second place, he would get sick of it. You should be one with your husband, but never in the shape of a parasite. He should be able to see growth in your soul, independent of him; and whenever he truly feels that he has received from you a stimulus to progress and to goodness, you have refreshed him, and made a great advance into his heart.

He should see that you really have a strong desire to make him happy, and to retain for ever the warmest place in his respect, his admiration, and his affection. Enter into all his plans with interest. Sweeten all his troubles with your sympathy. Make him feel that there is one ear always open to the revelation of his experiences, that there is one heart that never misconstrues him, that there is one refuge for him in all circumstances; and that in all wearinesses of body and soul, there is one warm pillow for his head, beneath which a heart is beating with the same unvarying truth and affection, through all gladness and sadness, as the faithful chronometer suffers no perturbation of its rhythm by shine or shower. A husband who has such a wife as this, has little temptation to spend much time away from home. He *cannot* stay away long at a time. He may "meet a man," but the man will not long detain him from his wife. He may go to "the post-office," but he will not call upon the friend's wife on the way. He can do better. The great danger is that he will love his home too well—that he will neither be willing to have you visit your aunts and cousins, nor, without a groan, accept an invitation to tea at your neighbor's.

But I leave this special point, to which I have devoted my space somewhat improvidently. There is one relation which you bear to your husband, or one aspect of your relation to him, to which I have not alluded sufficiently. You are not only the wife of his bosom—the object of his affections, but you have a business relation with him—you are his helpmate. To a very great extent you are dependent upon him, but you are also his assistant,—bound to use his money economically, and to aid, so far as you can, in saving and accumulating it. The woman who feels that she has a right to spend every cent that "the old man" allows her, and that all she gets out of him is hers to lavish upon her vanities, takes a very low view of her relations to him. It is simply the view of a mistress, and is utterly dishonorable—utterly mercenary. The money which he puts into your hand endows you simply with a stewardship. You have no right to waste it, or to part with it, for anything but such values as are consistent with his means. You have consented to be the partner of his life, and you have no more right to squander his money than his business partner has. It is your duty to husband it; and happy are you if your companion has such confidence in your faithfulness to him and his interest, that he puts money into your hand always willingly, believing that it will be parted with judiciously, and with discreet and conscientious regard to his means and abilities. If your husband has no confidence in your economy and discretion, and consequently stints you, and absolutely feels obliged to place you in the position of a favorite dependent and pensioner—a play thing or a housekeeper for whom he has got to pay—you are not happy by any means.

You can do very much in your character of helpmate to lighten your husband's cares, and relieve him from anxieties. If he finds you looking closely after his interests, buying economically the food for his table, and never wastefully sacrificing your old dresses in consequence of your thirst for new, always counting the cost of every object which you may desire, you relieve his mind from a load of care which no man can carry without embarrassment. A man who feels that there is in his own house a leak which will absorb all he may earn, be that little or much, and that he has got to suffer it, and suffer from it, or institute restrictions that will probably make him appear mean in the eyes of his wife (wasteful wives are very apt to have mean husbands) the great stimulus and encouragement of his industry are taken away from him.

The full appreciation of your character, as your husband's helpmate, depends upon the thorough identification of yourself with him. Of this I have talked before, and call it up again for the purpose of showing you that there is absolutely no aspect of your relation to him which can be considered legitimate and complete that does not involve his identification. It is an equal thing. You are interested in your husband's expenditures; and he is interested in yours. You have cast in your lot together—your whole lot; and he has no more right to expend his money in such a way as to embarrass you and deprive you of what you need, than you have to squander the means which he places at your disposal. It is a partnership concern, and if you succeed in managing your department of it in such a way as to secure your husband's confidence, fairly considering the cost of every cent to him, he will feel that he is appreciated, honored, and loved. Very likely he will understand this better than tasteful comforts and tender demonstrations of a lighter nature—demonstrations that involve no self-denial.

LETTER IV.

THE REARING OF CHILDREN

Once thou wert hidden in her painful side,
A boon unknown, a mystery and a fear;
Strange pangs she bore for thee; but HE whose name
Is everlasting LOVE hath healed her pain;
And paid her suffering hours with living joy.

HENRY ALFORD

Hail, wedded Love! mysterious law; true source
Of human offspring!

MILTON.

MY theory of life is that it is a school of mental and moral development—that God intended that each soul should pass under a series of influences, whose office it should be to evolve all its faculties, and soften and harmonize them. To this end, he has laid upon each a sweet necessity to adopt the ordinances he has contrived. When I speak of necessity, I do not mean compulsion, save in a limited sense—compulsion entirely consistent with individual election. Thus I believe that there is a very material portion of mental and moral development which cannot be achieved out of the marriage relation; and, to bring men and women into this relation, he has given them the sentiment of love, and the desire of mutual personal possession. This sentiment and desire are made so strong that they may hardly be resisted, so that all shall choose to be joined in conjugal relations. Thus the strong are softened by the weak, and the weak are invigorated by the strong; and the influences of men and women upon each other become the most powerful agencies for their mutual harmonious growth. But this is not all. When a pair have become united in wedlock, there rises in each healthy heart a desire for offspring. Nothing is more natural than this desire, and nothing more imperative. Its germ is seen far back in childhood. The boy's love of pets is but a manifestation of the primary outreachings of this desire, which fasten at first upon the only possible objects; and there probably never lived a little girl that did not love her doll beyond all other playthings. She takes it first, and retains it the longest of any.

This brings me to the subject of children, as legitimately something to be talked about in these letters. The having and the rearing of children form one of

God's ordinances for making you what you should be—what he wishes you to be. They are as necessary to you as you are to them. You can no more reach the highest and most harmonious development of which you are capable without children, than you can develop a muscle without exercise. Without them, one of the most beautiful regions of your nature must for ever remain without appropriate and direct culture. The offices of children in the culture of their parents are manifold. In the first place, they are a conservative and regulating force. A pair living together without children naturally become selfish. A pair unwatched by innocent eyes are often thrown off their guard in their language towards, and treatment of, each other. They lose one great stimulus to industry, and do not possess that which is, perhaps, the strongest bond, under all the circumstances of life, which can bind husband and wife together. There can be no true development of heart and mind where pure selfishness is the predominant principle; so God ordains that in each house there shall be little ones, more precious than all else, who shall engage the sympathy, tax the efforts, and absorb the love of those who sustain to them the relation of parents. The law is irreversible that our best individual progress in mental and moral good shall be attained by efforts devoted to others; and in children, each parent finds the nearest objects of such devotion. And there is, perhaps, nothing which so tends to soften the heart, to develop the kindlier affections, and to unlock and chasten the sympathies of men and women, as the children which sit around their table, and frolic upon their knees.

When I see a man stop in the streets to comfort some weeping child, or to get a kiss from a pair of juvenile lips, I know that he has passed through a blessed experience with children. A helpless little head has been laid upon his shoulder, in some hushed and hallowed room where the great mystery of birth has been enacted. Some feeble, wailing boy, pressed to his breast, has been borne, night after night, with weary arms, back and forth in the dimly lighted chamber, while the mother caught her short half hours of rest. More likely still, some precious warbler, her eyes closed, her lips for ever stilled, her golden curls parted away from a marble forehead, a white rose in her hand, has been laid in the grave, and the sod that covers her has been fertilized by his tears. Oh! there is something in loving dependent children, in tender care for them, and in losing them, even, which bestows upon the soul the most enriching of its experiences. They make us tender and sympathetic, and a thousand times reward us for all we do for them. We cannot get along without them; you cannot get along without them. You cannot afford to do it. They are cheap at the price of pain and sickness, and care and toil.

What do I mean by talk like this? What do I mean by the utterance of common-place like this? I mean simply to reveal some of the considerations upon which I condemn a great and growing vice among the young married people of this country—a vice which involves essential murder in many instances, and swells the profits of a thousand nostrum venders. And what do I mean by this? I mean that in thousands of American homes children have come to be regarded either as nuisances or luxuries. I mean that, in these homes, to have children is deemed a great misfortune. They are the bugbear that threatens people away from the marriage relation, and frightens them when in it. I mean that men and women, more and more in this country, hug to themselves their selfish delights, cherish their selfish ease, and consult their selfish convenience, without a consideration of their duties as men and women and without a comprehension of the fact that they can only find their highest enjoyment by obedience to the laws of God, natural and revealed. I mean that there are multitudes who envy those unblest with children, and congratulate them upon their poverty. I mean tha there are husbands who grudge every charm lost btheir wives in the duties and sacrifices of maternity, and that there are wives who are made spiteful and angry by the interference of children with their indolent habits, their love of freedom and self-indulgence, and their vain pursuits. I mean that the number i increasing of those who receive the choicest earthly blessings God can confer with ingratitude and wilful complainings. That is precisely what I mean; and I do not hesitate to say that it is all a very shabby and sinful thing, and that it is high time that those who are guilty were ashamed of it.

A woman who, by cool and calculating choice, is no mother, and who congratulates herself that she has no "young ones" tied to her apron strings, is either very unfortunately organized, or she is essentially immoral. A man who can tip up his feet, over against his lonely wife, and thank his stars that he has no "squalling brats" around to bother him, is a brute. It is time that some one protest, and I hereby do protest, against one of the great sins and shames of the age,—a sin which deadens the conscience, bestializes the affections, and ruins the health of the mistaken creatures who practise it,—which cuts the channel from one end of the land to the other of a broader Ganges than that which bubbles along its heathenish bank with the expiring breath of infancy.

There is growing up a cowardly disposition to shirk trouble and responsibility in this matter. "I don't feel competent to bring up a family of children." Who does? It is a part of your education to acquire competence for this work. "But I don't feel like assuming such a responsibility." That responsibility is precisely what you need to keep you in the path you ought to walk in. "But I can't afford it." Are there two pairs of hands between you, and not sufficient patience, courage, and enterprise to do the duties of life? "But I am afraid that I should lose my children. They are liable to so many accidents that it would be very strange if I should be able to raise a family without losing one or two." The sweetest and truest couplet that the Queen's laureate ever wrote tells the story upon this point:—

> "'Tis better to have loved and lost
> Than never to have loved at all."

Ask the father and the mother, weeping over the coffin of their first-born and only child, whether they regret that the child was born. Ask them the same question in after years, when that little life has come to be a thread of gold running through all their experiences. If they give an affirmative answer, I will be silent. No, my married friends—you who shrink from accepting the choicest privilege bestowed upon you—you are all wrong; and if you live, you will arrive at a period where you will see that there are rewards and punishments attached to this thing. What is to sustain you when, in old age—the charms of youth all past, desire extinguished, and the grasshopper a burden—you sit at your lonely board, and think of the strangers who are to enjoy the fruit of your most fruitless life? Who are to feed the deadening affections of your heart and keep life bright and desirable to its close, but the little ones whom you rear to manhood and womanhood? What is to reward you for the toils of life if you do not feel that you—your thoughts, your blood, your influence—are to be continued into the future? Do you like the idea of having hirelings, or those who are anxious to get rid of you, about your dying bed? Is it not worth something to have a family of children whom you have reared, lingering about your grave, with tears on their cheeks and blessings on their lips—tears for a great loss, and blessings on the hallowed influence which has trained them in the path of duty, and directed them to life's noblest ends?

This is a subject which has not been talked about *much publicly, but it is a very serious thing with* me, and it ought to be with you. I love the family life. I esteem a Christian family—the more numerous the better—one of the most beautiful subjects of contemplation the earth affords. A father, thoroughly chastened and warmed in all his affections, and a mother overflowing with love for the dear children God has given her devoted to their welfare, and guiding them by her tender counsels, sitting at their board with the sprightly forms and bright eyes of childhood around the table, or all kneeling at the family altar, form a sight more nearly allied to heaven than any other which the world presents. Do you suppose such a father would be what he is but for his children? Do you believe such a mother would be the blessed being she is but for the development which she receives in her maternal office? No, you know that both have been chastened, elevated, purified, made strong, and essentially glorified, by a relation as sanctifying as it is sacred.

So I say, in closing, that you can never realize the very choicest and richest blessings that Heaven intends for you, in your relations as husband and wife, without children. Whom God deprives of these, he has other thought for, and I have nothing to say to them; but to the multitude, I say, give welcome to each new comer whom God has lighted with a spark of his own divinity, to grow in glory till it shall outshine the star beneath which it entered existence, such greeting as you would give an angel. Clothe him in white, bear him to the baptismal font, rejoice over him as a testimonial that God remembers you, and celebrate the day when he was given to your arms in such a manner that he shall know that it is a blessed thing to be born. Sing to him plea sant songs, and scatter roses upon his cradle. "Of such is the kingdom of heaven," and in such the Saviour has given to you those to whose pure, simple, and innocent likeness he would have you conform your heart. You are to rear your boy to manhood, and educate him to be a man; and he, in turn, is to educate you to be a child, and protect your helpless years. It is an even thing, and a beautiful exhibition of that wonderful machinery by which all are made to bear equal burden in evolving the noblest life of the race.

LETTER V.

SEPARATION—FAMILY RELATIVES—SERVANTS.

Whate'er the uplooking soul admires,
Whate'er the senses' banquet be,
Fatigues, at last, with vain desires,
Or sickens by satiety.

But, truly, my delight was more
In her to whom I'm bound for aye
Yesterday than the day before,
And more to-day than yesterday!

THE ANGEL IN THE HOUSE.

THERE are so many subjects which call for notice in my letters to you that one letter, at least, must be a piece of patchwork. I propose that this one shall bear such a character.

It is doubtless a general experience that a husband and wife, after living together for a time, become in a measure tired of one another's company Before marriage, they were essential to each other; after long months of intimacy, a sense of monotony creeps upon them, and a separation for a few weeks is regarded as desirable, or not to be regretted. The husband would like a little more freedom; the wife, perhaps, pines for the associations of her free and careless girlhood. When this feeling comes upon a married pair, the time for a temporary separation has arrived, and the quicker it is instituted the better. The object and end of it is to prove to both that they cannot be happy when separated. The first week will pass off very pleasantly; the second will find them rather longing for one another's society again; the third will burden the mails with tender epistles in which the romance and ardor of courtship will be revived; the fourth will convince the wife that she has the very dearest husband in the world, and the husband will carry his package of letters in his breast pocket and sigh; the fifth will find a day set for the greatly longed-for re-union, about which both will be thinking all the time; and the sixth will bring the wife home, with all her precious beauty and band-boxes; and such a meeting will take place as well might make an observing old bachelor commit suicide. Well, they have learned a lesson which they will remember as long as they shall live. It is proved to them that they cannot be happy apart, and that separation will always be a calamity.

Various circumstances spring up in the course of life which seem to dictate a temporary separation, on the score of economy or profit. A man will desire to go into a distant city, for a sojourn of months and perhaps years, that he may buy and sell and get gain. The wife may not go, as it would interfere with the profits. This is one case; and there may be a thousand others in which policy dictates a like temporary separation. My counsel is to regard all such inducements for separation as temptations of the devil. It is morally degrading for a husband and wife to live apart from each other. It is the rupture of a sacred tie—the denial of a sacred pledge—the breaking up of a relation into which religion, affection, and habits of thought and life have all become intimately interwoven, leaving both man and woman loosely floating among new influences, and freed from the restraints to which their lives had become conformed.

Separation for the time being destroys the comfort and withholds the rewards of married life. It is a long, dreary, monotonous, or anxious episode, for which neither fame nor money can compensate. It is this, or worse; for, certainly, nothing can compensate for the acquisition of that indifference on either side which proves that separation is not a calamity. A broken bone, too long left without setting, can never again make a firm junction. Separation which shows that a pair cannot live apart is well; separation which proves that they can, is one of the worst things that can happen. Therefore I say to every man, that the circumstances should be most extraordinary which will leave him at liberty to break up his home, or justify him in separating from his wife. If you cannot take the wife of your bosom with you, you are to believe, generally, that your plans have not the favor of Providence.

It is the habit of some husbands and wives to have intimate friends whom they cherish and correspond with, independently. I have known very good husbands to carry on limited flirtations with girls, to be the repositories of secrets belonging to such, and to act as their very agreeable next friends. Very pleasant connexions are these, to a young husband, who has time to attend to them, but very dangerous in the long run. Similar connexions on the other side of the house have made a great deal of difficulty since the world began. They are very harmless things at first; but there is nothing but danger in the intimacy of a married heart with an unmarried one, unless there be other relationships which justify it. A man or a woman who, from the most innocent motives originally, plays with such an intimacy as this, is toying with a very dangerous instrument. It leads to the establishment of secrets between husband and wife—itself a bad thing—and too frequently leads to their estrangement, more or less pronounced. You should never write a letter, or give occasion for the receipt of one, which you are unwilling to show to your companion. Under none but extraordinary circumstances should you consent to receive a secret from a friend which he or she may be unwilling your companion should know.

If you have friends, they should be the friends of your companion; and this should be carried outside of the circle of your intimacies. You have no business with a friend who refuses to be your companion's friend; and again you have no business with a friend whom, for a valid reason, your companion refuses to know. You may have come together from different classes of society The wife or the husband may be proscribed by a class while her or his companion may be a favorite of the same class. A husband or a wife, who is willing to ignore his proscription and distinction, demonstrates a lack of spirit and self-respect that is utterly contemptible. A husband or a wife acting thus dishonors his or her own flesh and blood. You go together; you are to be received together or not at all; and an insult to one is an insult to both, always, and under all circumstances.

And now that I have spoken of your mutual relations to intimates and friends, it is proper that I speak of your relations to your respective blood connexions. Very fruitful causes of disturbance between husbands and wives are the relatives of the married pair. Not unfrequently the parents of the husband are brought into his family, and not unfrequently those of the wife. Doubtless there are instances in which it is impossible to get along without difficulty with these, but if you have fully apprehended my course of reasoning with you, and admitted its validity, there is but one course for you to pursue. You are one. The husband's parents are the wife's parents, and the wife's parents are the parents of the husband. You are to receive and treat them as your own—not with constraint and as a matter of duty, but willingly and affectionately. You are to learn to love and respect them,—to bear with their frailties, to comfort them in their passage to the tomb, to treat them in no sense as dependents, and to make them feel that they are not only welcome to your kindly offices, but that they have a right to the home which they have with you. You are young, and they are old. It is for the honor of your companion that his or her parents have support at his or her hands, and what is your companion's honor is yours. Besides, this world is a world of compensations, more nicely adapted and more certain than you know. The time will pass away, and the children now on your knee will have grown to manhood and womanhood, and will have chosen their companions as their fathers and mothers chose theirs before them The home which you now enjoy may be broken up Your companion will be taken from you, and your only resort may be the home of your child. The treatment which you would wish to receive from your son's wife, or your daughter's husband, is precisely the treatment which you now owe to those who hold to you the relation which you will then sustain to them.

The same rules which govern you in regard to the parents should extend to the circle of your other relatives. Of course, your ability to maintain dependents is a consideration; but I regard personal and family honor as most inseparably involved in this thing. A son or a daughter who, with the power of maintaining without impossible self-sacrifice a father and mother, allows them to finish their life in an alms-house, or to live on the charity of those upon whom they have no pecial claims, is a brute. There are a few such miserable creatures in the world, who ought to be hooted at and cut by all decent people. In a measure the same thing is true of all family relatives. It is a matter of personal and family pride, as I have said. It is something more than this. The poor we have always with us, and we owe a duty to them, unless we ourselves are equally poor; but when a man has poor relatives who must be dependent, more or less, upon some one, it is as if God's finger had kindly pointed out to him the very objects upon which his benefactions should be bestowed.

I am aware that this is rather serious doctrine for some minds. I am aware that relatives are often proud as well as poor; that they will be dependent rather than labor; that they become insufferable drones and bores, and haunt your homes with a most offensive and vexatious presence. There ought to be some short method of treating such, but I do not possess it. If you cannot make them useful, there are several ways of making them uncomfortable which may be safely left to the invention and discretion of the suffering parties. My plea is for a thorough identification of family feeling and family pride between husband and wife. If it entail disagreeable and unjust burdens, through the laziness or extravagance of dependent relatives, it is a misfortune; but misfortunes are incident to all relations. Better bear them than leave your motives open to suspicion, or bring disgrace upon your family name.

I cannot close this letter better than by saying a word or two upon the subject of servants. The general proposition that the quality of the servant is dependent upon the quality of the mistress is a sound one. If a woman who frets at and scolds her servants ever has a good servant, it is in spite of the treatment she receives. In order to be a good mistress, it is necessary to believe in a few fundamental truths, which may be briefly stated as follows: *First*, servants are human beings, and consequently have souls; *second*, servants, having souls, are consequently controlled by the motives which address themselves to a common humanity; *third*, being human, servants have rights which no amount of service money can buy; and *fourth*, transcendent intellectual endowments, a physical development of fifty-horse power, the broad circle of the Christian graces and virtues, a faultless disposition, a knowledge of French cookery, and elegant habits, cannot be obtained for nine Yankee shillings a week. A mistress admitting generally the truth of these propositions possesses a basis for securing service that shall be reasonably satisfactory to her.

There is quite too much of the feeling among mistresses that they have a right to use a servant as a fast boy uses a hired horse. They are to get the most out of them that they can for the money they pay. They take no personal interest in them,—extend to them no matronly care and kindness. They forget that a servant is a social being. They forget that she has humble loves and hopes, has desires for freedom and recreation, as important to her as the higher love and hopes and desires of the more favored girls who occupy the parlor. They forget that the labors of the kitchen are tedious; that the confinement of the kitchen is irksome. They become exacting,—strict in rules, rigid in discipline, and peremptory in their commands. It is not in human nature to stand this kind of thing, so the servant gets hardened at last, or wilfully careless. She receives no praise, any way, and therefore tries to get none. A servant, generally speaking, whose feelings as a humble woman are appreciated by her mistress, who is praised for what she does that is well, and kindly and patiently instructed to correct that which is not well; who is treated to sympathetic and considerate words, and indulged in that liberty which is absolutely essential to her bodily and mental health, will love her mistress, and have a desire to please. This, in all good and tolerably sensible natures, will settle the matter. A girl exercised by this love and this desire will be a good servant ninety-nine times in a hundred. It is under relations like these that attachments are formed which are as tender as humanity and as lasting as life.

There is a broad view in which this and all kindred matters are to be regarded. The mistress is quite as dependent upon the servant as the servant upon the mistress. She renders an equivalent for what you give her, and her service is as essential to you as your money is to her. You cannot get along without her, nor can she get along without you. Your position, to be sure, is superior to hers, but she owes you nothing, save faithful service and respect. The obligations are not al upon one side. It is just as much your duty to be a kind mistress and friend to her, as it is her duty to give faithful service and respectful treatment to you. If, therefore, you fail in your duty, you must not blame her for failing in hers. I have never yet seen a good servant who had not either a good mistress, or one who was actually inferior to herself. Human nature is very prevalent among women, and especially among maids of all-work.

LETTER VI.

THE INSTITUTION OF HOME.

Home of our childhood! How affection clings,
And hovers round thee with her seraph wings!

O. W. HOLMES.

For there are two heavens, sweet,
Both made of love—one inconceivable
Even by the other, so divine it is;
The other far on this side of the stars
By men called HOME, when some blest pair have met,
As we are now.

LEIGH HUNT.

THE French have no word into which the English word *home* may be legitimately translated; yet it is sufficiently evident that many of the French people have the thing without the name, while a large portion of the American people have the name without the thing. There are comparatively few who have an adequate idea of what home is, as an institution. It is recognised as a house, containing a convenient number of chairs and tables, with a sufficiency of chamber furniture and eatables, a place to eat and sleep in, simply. It is not unjust to say that half of the young married people of America have no higher conception of home than this. What they call their homes are simply boarding-houses, where, for purposes of economy and convenience, they board themselves.

In my idea, home rises to the dignity of an institution of life, and, like everything legitimately to be called an institution of life, is both an outgrowth of life, and a contributor to its development. Like all institutions, it has its external form and internal power and significance. Like the church, it has its edifice and appointments not only, but its membership, its bonds of spiritual fellowship, and its germinal ideas, developing themselves into influences that bear flowers and fruits to charm and feed the soul. It is into the meaning of the word HOME that I would introduce you first, my friends, and then into the home itself. Marriage is the legitimate basis of a genuine home. A husband is its priest and a wife its priestess; and it is for you, young husband and young wife, to establish this institution, maintain it, beautify it in its outward form, fill it with all good influences, develope its capacities, make it the expression of your best ideas of intimate social life, and to use it as an instrument of genial power in moulding such outside life as may come into contact with it. Its outward form and its internal arrangements should, so far as your means will permit, be the outgrowth of your finest ideas and the expression of your best tastes, combined with the practical ingenuities which may be rendered necessary by a wholesome economy.

It is not the elm before the door of home that the sailor pines for when tossing on the distant sea. It is not the house that sheltered his childhood, the well that gave him drink, nor the humble bed where he used to lie and dream. These may be the objects that come to his vision as he paces the lonely deck, but the heart within him longs for the sweet influences that came through all these things, or were associated with them; for the heart clings to the institution which developed it—to that beautiful tree of which it is the fruit. Wherever, therefore, the heart wanders, it carries the thought of home with it. Wherever, by the rivers of Babylon, the heart feels its loss and loneliness, it hangs its harp upon the willows and weeps. It prefers home to its chief joy. It will never forget it. For there swelled its first throb. There were developed its first affections. There a mother's eyes looked into it; there a mother's voice spoke to it; there a mother's prayers blessed it. There the love of parents and brothers and sisters gave it precious entertainment. There bubbled up from unseen fountains life's first effervescing hopes. There life took form, and color, and consistence. From that centre went out all its young ambitions. Toward that focus return its concentring memories. There it took form, and fitted itself to loving natures and pleasant natural scenes; and it will carry that impress wherever it may go, unless it become perverted by sin or make to itself another home, sanctified by a new and more precious affection.

It is in the little communities which we call American homes that the hope of America rests. It is here that subordination to wholesome restraint and respect for law are inculcated. It is here, if anywhere, that the affections receive their culture, that amiable dispositions are developed, that the amenities of life are learned, that the mind and the body are established in healthful habits, that mutual respect for mutual rights is engendered, and here that all those faculties and qualities are nurtured which enter into the structure of worthy character. In the homes of America are born the children of America, and from them go out into American life American men and women. They go out with the stamp of these homes upon them, and only as these homes are what they should be, will they be what they should be. It is with this in view that I offer a few suggestions touching the establishment of this institution by you.

Just as soon as it is possible for you to do so, buy a house, the ground it stands on, and as much land around it as your business, convenience, or taste may require. A home can never be all that it should be to you and yours, unless you own it. This is doubtless impossible to a great multitude who will read this letter, but let not such be discouraged. A beautiful home life may be developed, even by a tenant at will; though the security and fixedness of proprietorship are greatly tributary to home's permanent influences. If the home is owned, see that its exterior represent you faithfully. What you cannot afford in architecture, you can supply in vines and flowers. The interior should receive the impress of all the order, neatness, taste, and ingenuity that are in you. Your home is the temple of your sweetest human love. It is in this temple that young immortals are born. It is here that characters are shaped into manhood and womanhood—the highest earthly estate. It is here that you are to work out the problem of your lives. It is a place of dignity. Therefore give it honor; make it beautiful; make it worthy!

All this, however, only relates to the location—the shell of your home. The ordering of its internal life is of still greater importance. The greatest danger of home life springs from its familiarity. Kindred hearts, gathered at a common fireside, are far too apt to relax from the proprieties of social life. Careless language and careless attire are too apt to be indulged in when the eye of the world is shut off, and the ear of the world cannot hear. I counsel no stiffness of family etiquette—no sternness of family discipline—like that which prevailed in the olden time. The day is past for that, but the day for thorough respectfulness among the members of a home—the day for careful propriety of dress and address—will never pass. For it is here that the truest and most faultless social life is to be lived; it is here that such a life is to be learned. A home in which politeness reigns is a home from which polite men and women go out; and they go out directly from no other.

The ordering of a home life is so intimately connected with the treatment of children, that this subject should be treated definitely. First, every child born to you should learn among the first things it is capable of learning, that in your home your will is supreme. The earlier a child learns this, the better; and he should learn, at the same time, from all your words and all your conduct, that such authority is the companion of the tenderest love and the most genial kindness. Play with your children as much as you please; make yourselves their companions and sympathizers and confidants; but keep all the time the reins of your authority steadily drawn, and never allow yourselves to be trifled with. It is only in this way that you can keep the management of your home in your own hands, and retain the affectionate respect of those whom you love as you do yourselves.

Again, make your home a happy place—a pleasant place. Much can be done towards this end by beautifying it in the manner I have already pointed out. Much more can be done by providing food and amusement for the minds of your children. These minds you will find to be active, restless, and greedy for new impressions. This restlessness is a heaven-implanted impulse. You have neither the power nor the right to repress it; but it is your duty to give it direction, so far as possible, and to guide it to legitimate ends. You will find one of three things to be true of your children. They will be happy at home, or discontented at home, or they will seek for happiness away from home. In the ignorance of the nature of childhood on the part of parents has originated the ruin of millions of men and women. Bursting from an unnatural and irrational restraint, they have rushed from the release of parental authority to perdition; or, allowed to seek for happiness away from home and away from restraint, they have contracted habits which curse them and their parents while they live. So I tell you that the only way for you to save your children is to make a home so pleasant to them—to provide such grateful changes for their uneasy natures—as shall make their home the most delightful spot on earth, a spot to be loved while they live in it, and a spot to be recalled with grateful memories when they leave it. Profoundly to be commiserated is that child who looks back upon his home as upon a prison-house; upon his youth as a season of hardship; upon his parents as tyrants. If such a child ever become a good and genial man or woman, it will be in spite of a bad home.

I am well aware that the homes of America will not become what they should be until a true idea of life shall become more widely implanted. The worship of the dollar does more to degrade American homes and the life of those homes than anything—than all things—else. Utility is the God of almost universal worship. The chief end of life is to gather gold, and that gold is counted lost which hangs a picture upon the wall, which purchases flowers for the yard, which buys a toy or a book for the eager hand of childhood. Is this the whole of human life? Then it is a mean, meagre, and a most undesirable thing! A child will go forth from such a home as a horse will go from a stall—glad to find free air and a wider pasture. The influence of such a home upon him in after life will be just none at all, or nothing good. Thousands are rushing from homes like these every year. They crowd into cities. They crowd into villages. They swarm into all places where life is clothed with a higher significance; and the old shell of home is deserted by every bird as soon as it can fly. Ancestral homesteads and patrimonial acres have no sacredness; and when the father and the mother die, the stranger's money and the stranger's presence obliterate associations that should be among the most sacred of all things.

I would have you build up for yourselves and for your children a home which will never be lightly parted with—a home which shall be to all whose lives have been associated with it the most interesting and precious spot upon earth. I would have that home the abode of dignity, propriety, beauty, grace, love, genial fellowships and happy associations. Out from such a home I would have good influences flow into neighborhoods and communities. In such a home I would see noble ambitions taking root, and receiving all generous culture. And there I would see you, young husband and young wife, happy. Do not deprive yourselves of such influences as will come to you through an institution like this. No money can pay you for such a deprivation. No circumstances but those of utter poverty can justify you in denying these influences to your children.

It is to the institution of home, as developed in its best form and power, under the letter and spirit of Christianity, that I point when the socialist approaches me with his sophisms, the New Lights with their loose theories of marriage, and the infidel with his howl over the basis of American civilization. It is the history of this home, since Christ lived, that is one of the strongest testimonials to his divine authority. In whatever land, under whatever system, by whatever men and women, the Christian home has been set aside for fanciful inventions, society has degenerated towards or into beastliness. As I have said before, the hope of America is the homes of America. If you to whom I write will each for himself and herself make these homes the noble institutions Heaven designs they shall be, this generation shall not pass away before the world shall look upon a people the like and the equal of which it has never seen. A generation shall take possession of the land full of dignity, love, grace, and goodness, glowing with a patriotism as true as their regard for home is sacred, and showing that the strength of the nation is forged under the smoke that rises from its happy household fires.

LETTER VII.

SOCIAL HOMES, AND BLESSINGS FOR DAILY USE.

How sweet, how passing sweet, is Solitude!
But grant me still a friend in my retreat
Whom I may whisper, Solitude is sweet!

COWPER.

The good he scorned,
Stalked off reluctant, like an ill used ghost,
Not to return.

ROBERT BLAIR.

I HAVE talked to you of your duties to each other, to your relatives, and to your servants. It remains to me to speak of your duties to society, as heads of families and rulers of homes.

I have insisted on the thorough identification of husband and wife in feeling, pride of character and family, pursuit, and interest; yet I am aware that this identification may be perverted into a most senseless and selfish devotion to one another, and an exclusiveness of communication, which are destructive of social life. I am acquainted with too many husbands and wives who, though all the world to each other, are nothing to th world. Their whole life is within their home. They gather comforts about them, they bear dainties to each other's lips; they live and move and have their whole being in each other's love; and, shutting out all the world, live only for themselves. I say I know too many such pairs as these. They are far too plenty. They cannot bear to be torn from their homes for an afternoon. They take no interest in others. They never call friends and neighbors around their board, and they consider it a hardship to fulfil the common offices of social politeness—to say nothing of hospitality. It is not unjust to say that this is one of the most dangerous and most repulsive forms of married life. It is selfishness doubled, associated, instituted; and it deserves serious treatment.

Homes, like individuals, have their relations to each other; and, as no man liveth to himself alone, no home should live to itself alone. It is through the medium of homes that the social life-blood of America is kept in circulation—through this medium almost exclusively. Every home should be as a city set upon a hill, that cannot be hid. Into it should flock friends and friendships, bringing the life of the world, the stimulus and the modifying power of contact with various natures, the fresh flowers of feeling gathered from wide fields. Out of it should flow benign charities, pleasant amenities, and all those influences which are the natural offspring of a high and harmonious home life. Intercommunication of minds and homes is the condition of individual and social development, and failing of this no married pair can be what they should be to each other. Exclusive devotion to business by day, and exclusive devotion to selfish home enjoyments at night, will dry up, harden, and depreciate the richest natures in the course of a few years; and, so soon as the man withdraws from the business of the world, the world has seen the last of him and his family for life. They have no outside associations. It is as if they did not live at all. When they die, nobody misses them, for they have been nothing to society. As many doors are open as before, and social life feels no ripple upon its surface when the sand is thrown upon their coffins.

There should glow in every house, throughout the land, the light of a pleasant welcome for friends. On every hearth should leap the flame that irradiates the forms and faces of associates. Neighborhood should mean something more than a collection of dark and selfishly-closed hearts and houses. A community should be something better than an aggregation of individuals and homes governed by the same laws, and sustaining equal civil burdens. Neighborhood should be the name of a vital relationship. A community should be a community in fact—informed with a genial, social life, in which the influence of each nature, the power of each intellect, the wealth of every individual acquisition, the force of every well-directed will, and the inspiration of every high and pure character, should be felt by all. A neighborhood of homes like this, would be a neighborhood indeed; and none other deserves the name.

The fact is, that selfishness is the bane of all life. It cannot enter into life—individual, family, or social—without cursing it. Therefore, if any married pair find themselves inclined to confine themselves to one another's society, indisposed to go abroad and mingle with the life around them, disturbed and irritated by the collection of friends in their own dwelling, or in any way moved to regard their social duties as disagreeable, let them be alarmed at once. It is a bad symptom—an essentially morbid symptom. They should institute means at once for removing this feeling; and they can only remove it by persistently going into society, persistently gathering it into their own dwelling, and persistently endeavoring to learn to love, and feel an interest in, all with whom they meet. The process of regeneration will not be a tedious one, for the rewards of social life are immediate. The heart enlarges quickly with the practice of hospitality. The sympathies run and take root, from point to point, each root throwing up leaves and bearing flowers and fruit like strawberry vines, if they are only allowed to do so. It is only sympathies and strawberries that are cultivated in hills, which do otherwise. The human face is a thing which should be able to bring the heart into blossom with a moment's shining, and it will be such with you, if you will meet it properly.

The penalties of family isolation will not, unhappily, fall entirely upon yourselves. They will be visited with double force upon your children. Children, reared in a home with few or no associations, will grow up either boorish or sensitively timid. It is a cruel wrong to children to rear them without bringing them into continued contact with polite social life. The ordeal through which children thus reared are obliged to pass, in gaining the ease and assurance which will make them at home elsewhere than under the paternal roof, is one of the severest; while those who are constantly accustomed to a social life from their youth, are educated in all its forms and graces without knowing it.

Great multitudes of men and women, all over the country, are now living secluded from social contact, simply from their sensitive consciousness of ignorance of the forms of graceful intercourse. They feel that they cannot break through their reserve. There is, doubtless, much that is morbid in this feeling, and yet it is mainly natural. From all this mortification and this deprivation, every soul might have been saved by education in a home where social life was properly lived. It is cruel to deny to children the opportunity, not only to become accustomed from their first consciousness to the forms of society, but to enjoy its influence upon their developing life. Society is food to children. Contact with other minds is the means by which they are educated; and the difference in families of children will show at once to the accustomed eye, the different social character of their parents. But I have no space to follow this subject further; and I leave it with you, with the earnest wish that you will consider it, and profit by the suggestions I have given you.

I must talk to you in this letter (for I have but one more to write) in regard to your way of living, and your main objects of life. Are you stretching every nerve and straining every muscle to get gold? Have you associated respectability with wealth? Are you denying to yourself a free and generous life now in your youth, in order to enjoy such a life when youth shall have passed away? Are you scrimping yourselves and your families by mean economies which grudge every sixpence that escapes you, and make of your life a hard and homely thing? I know of many young married people who are living a life like this, and I pity them more than I blame them, because they are victims of false ideas, very probably inculcated by thrifty parents or by most thriftless philosophers. If you are an unsocial pair, the probabilities are that you are engaged in precisely this business.

Now I wish to tell you of something very much better than this. I am not going to advise you to adopt a luxurious style of living. I am not going to tell you to spend all you get, and to run in debt for that which you are unable to pay for. But I say that for every capable and healthy man, and every clever and sensible woman, both of whom are industrious, there is enough to be won in the work of life to afford a generous living, and leave a sufficient margin for independent competence. The years of your life will be few, at the most; nd for you to throw away the enjoyment of their passing days for a good which may never come, to be enjoyed in a life that is uncertain, is to throw away for ever the blessings which God intends for your present food. God's blessings are not cumulative. The manna that fell in the wilderness came every day, and spoiled with the keeping. You may lay up wealth for age, but age, with its teeth gone, its sensibilities killed, and without employment, cannot enjoy it. So, I tell you to enjoy your wealth while you are earning it. I do not mean by this that you are to lay up nothing. I do no mean that you shall be imprudent or improvident. I only counsel that use of your money, from day to day, which will give you generous food, tasteful dress, and pleasant surroundings, and which will tend to make life comfortable and beautiful.

But some will read this who are in poverty, who do not hope to obtain even independence. I am not writing to you, my friends, but to your neighbors, less happy than you, who have taken it into their heads to get rich. Perhaps they may be your employers. At any rate, they are very unenviable people. I write to those who have the power to make money, and who ignore the present blessings of their lot—who enjoy no present blessings. I write to those who wait for wealth to make their first contributions to public charities, to aid in the support of social and religious institutions, to mingle in that neighborhood life which involves a genial hospitality, to fill their library with books and their halls with pictures, to resort to the concert and exhibition rooms for refining amusement, to give employment to the poor, to make their homes the embodiment of good taste and substantial comfort, and to provide for health and pleasant recreation.

I believe that twice as much may be enjoyed in this life, as is now enjoyed, if people would only take and use the blessings which Heaven confers on them for present use. We strive to accumulate beyond our wants, and beyond the wants of our families. In doing this, we deny to ourselves leisure, recreation, culture, and social relaxation. When wealth has been won, our power to enjoy it is past, and it goes into the hands of children whose industry and enterprise it kills and whose best life it spoils. It is not often that great accumulations of wealth do anybody good. They usually spoil the happiness of two generations—one in the getting, and one in the spending.

I love the man who earns his money with the special design of spending it—the man who regards money only as a means of procuring that which shall supply the passing wants of his nature—of his whole nature—and for securing education to his children, and comfort to his old age. It is to such that men go for subscriptions to worthy objects. It is by the fireside and at the board of such that I am happy. It is with the free and generous souls of such that I delight to come in contact. It is for such souls that life is made. Such men as these go on from year to year, building up their homes, making them abodes of beauty and plenty, and places of refreshment for five hundred cordial hearts. Wherever they go, hands of warm good fellows are held out to them. They have the blessing of the helpless, and the envy of no man. Sometimes, perhaps, their wives are envied by the wives of other men, but it is probably out of the power of either party to help that.

LETTER VIII.

A VISION OF LIFE AND ITS MEANING.

Here manhood struggles for the sake
Of mother, sister, daughter, wife,
The graces and the loves which make
The music of the march of life;
And woman, in her daily round
Of duty, walks on holy ground!

WHITTIER.

And so, 'twixt joy,
And love, and tears, and whatsoever pain
Man fitly shares with man, these two grow old;
And, if indeed blest thoroughly, they die
In the same spot, and nigh the same good hour;
And setting suns look heavenly on their grave!

LEIGH HUNT.

THIS is my twenty-fourth and last letter to the young. As a preliminary to its composition, I have re-read every previous letter, and the subject of this has been suggested by the perusal. I have asked myself "what kind of men and women will these letters make, if there happen to be any who adopt their counsels?" The reply comes to me in the form of a vision which I will unfold to you.

I see a young man standing at the opening gates o life, and with earnest eyes scanning the landscape that stretches before him. Flowers are springing at his feet among the velvet grass; brooks are dragging their chains of flashing silver over the rocks, and passing in careless frolic towards the sea; birds are fluttering like wind-tossed blossoms amid the overhanging foliage, and breathing their fragrant melody upon the air; breezes full of love are fanning his cheek, and filling him with a sense of intoxicating pleasure, and the sky is bending over him with no break of blue save where, in the exalted perspective, golden clouds sit like crowns upon golden mountains. His heart is bold, his limbs are strong, his blood is healthful, and his whole susceptible and sensuous nature throbs with responses to the appeals of the beauty and music and sweetness around and before him.

He takes a step, and Pleasure comes from her secret bower, and invites him to her banquet of delights. He pauses for a moment, shivers with the stress of the temptation, puts her resolutely aside, and passes on. Idleness, lolling beneath a shade, points to a vacant seat, and closes her languid eyes; but with disgust he leaves her and presses forward. Ambition beckons from some sudden summit, but he heeds her not. Then Duty comes, and standing before him—a firm and earnest figure—points to a burden and bids him take it up, and bear it as he journeys onward. He pauses, looks around, ahead, above, then lifts it to his shoulder, and with muscles firmly strained presses forward with new vigor. Soon he becomes accustomed to the load, and then Duty comes again, and bids him add to it. He willingly takes on the new burden, and as he does so, finds his heart warming with cheerfulness, and his voice bursting into song. Revellers, steeped with wine and wild with hilarity, look up from their vine-covered table at the sound of the healthy lay, and laugh and scoff, but they do not approach him. Temptations that throng the path of the weak and faithless slink away from him without attack; or, if one scatter its charms upon him, they slide off like dew from bronze.

So Duty becomes to him a guiding angel. Wherever she leads he follows. In her steps he drops into deep ravines, hidden from the light of the sun; he plunges into streams whose billows affright and chill him, and crosses them by a might which grows with every struggle; he scales mountains that lie in his path, piled with huge discouragements, and sees from the summit of achievement, shimmering in the distance, the streams of great reward, winding among meadows of heavenly recompense. At last he comes to a point in his way where he pauses, and looks around him. In the pause, he listens to the beating of his own heart. It is the thrill and rhythm of manhood which that heart is strongly telling. He sees that he has made progress towards the golden mountains, with their crowns of golden clouds. The noise of the revellers has died upon his ear. Pleasure and Indolence are far back, and the temptations of youth are past, and he is, so far, safe. He sees how the burdens he has borne and the struggles he has put forth have knit his muscles, and strengthened his will, and developed his power. He sees how each constituent of the manhood that has now become his choicest possession was won by toil and fatigue, and self-denial and patience and resistance of temptation. He sees that it could have been won in no other way, and gives honest thanks to the Providence which has thus transmuted the evil of life into good.

There we leave him standing, and change the scene. At another gate a maiden enters. The rose sits upon her cheek, and the lily upon her bosom. Good angels are hovering all about her; and seeking some secret recess, she kneels and dedicates herself to Heaven. As she comes into the path, the Tempter looks at her, and slinks away from her sweet and unsuspicious eyes, as if they were windows through which he had caught a glimpse of God. She is conscious from the first that life has meaning in it, and that the soul which informs her has a duty and a destiny. She knows that that soul is to be strengthened and enriched,—that it is to be kept pure, and beautified with all precious graces. Fashion and Frivolity flaunt their gewgaws before her eyes, but she puts them aside. They seek to divert her into vain pursuits, but she has a steady purpose and keeps a steady path. Flocks of seductive thoughts hover about her head, and tease her bewildered eyes; but she repels them until they leave her. She gathers the flowers of life that bloom by the way, and places them in her hair. Kind words and smiles go out from her, and come back winged blessings to nestle on her breast. Little deeds of charity and mercy, dropped by the way, change into pearls, and seek her hand again. The mother leans upon her shoulder, and the sister clings to her arm. Up weary slopes she toils to gather fruits from the tree of knowledge. Down into valleys of suffering she walks, bearing balsams for the sick. She thinks of ease but to scorn it, and finds in the exercise of her faculties and the play of her sympathies and the development of her powers such healthful joy as only the worthy know. And thus she passes on—a creature of beauty, a bearer of purity, a being of modest graces and noble aptitudes, of fine instincts and self-denying heroism, until her nature brims—a golden goblet—with the wine of womanhood, and she meets the companion for whom God designed her—whom God designed for her.

Thus our third scene is prepared for us. Manhood and womanhood meet, and lives that were separate melodies become a harmony. How it may seem to others I know not, but true love between man and woman—the love that gives its all for life, for the simple rewards of congenial companionship, seems to me the most lovely outgrowth of human nature. God and all good things breathe benisons upon it. It is the advent of a heart into another heart,—the entrance of one spiritual nature into the spiritual nature of another, giving, I doubt not, a foretaste of the exquisite bliss which thrills the soul as it passes into the gate of Paradise. And there stand our young man and young woman, her head upon his shoulder, and her ear drinking in the tender confessions of an affection to which her happy heart responds in gentlest numbers. "What God hath joined together let no man put asunder," falls from the sky where the evening star is glowing. They look up, and a pledge, heard in heaven and on earth, falls from their lips. Friends flock around them, and kisses fall upon the young wife's cheek amid the baptism of tears. Golden fruits are borne to their lips, and the twilight air is full of the pleasant jargon of happy human voices. Oh! brightly gleam the golden mountains in the last rays of the sunken sun; and the golden clouds that crown them blaze with more than a solar glory.

And now begins the united life. Hand in hand and heart to heart they resume their passage up the long incline. In the early morning, I see them kneeling side by side, worshipping the God of their life, confessing their weakness and their sin, and praying for that spiritual nourishment which shall build them up into a saintly estate. At evening, before they lie down by the wayside for repose, I see them kneel again, and commune with the Good Father whose spirit dwells within them. If one takes up a cross, it is lightened by the other's hand. If one gathers a joy from the boughs of Heaven's munificence, the other is called to share it. With no heart-wanderings, no untruth, no repinings, no selfish monopoly of delight, they pass on for months till now I see that the wife has become a mother, and bears a little babe upon her bosom. It is a gift of God, precious beyond all price; and when they kneel again they thank God for it,—for all the joy it brings them, for all the care it imposes upon them, for all the hallowed sympathies it calls into play, for the new springs of pleasure and life which it uncovers to them. Soon the little one is on its feet, and dances along the way, while another takes its place in the maternal arms. And as the years pass away, another and another are added to the pilgrim group, till they look like a band of attendant cherubim.

Meanwhile, I see that the limbs of the pair are growing weary. The way is hard and rough, and both are laden with a burden of care, accumulating as they go; and now they pass into a cloud. Dimly through the vapor gathering before my own eyes, or enveloping them, I see them bowing by the way. One of the little ones—its fingers full of life's roses—lies stretched upon the sand. They kiss his marble cheek, and the little group bend over him and weep trickling tears, like statues at a fountain. I hear the mother say—"Oh, but for these, would I had died for thee, my son!" From the far height I hear the tone of a bell:—is it on earth or in heaven? Is it a sad bell or a glad bell? I know not; but I see that after they have hollowed a little grave, and deposited their treasure, and knelt upon it and said, "Thy will, not mine," the cloud is drunk up by the unseen spirits of the air, and away, on the pinnacle of the golden mountains, stands a little form with its fingers full of roses, beckoning! There is a stir in the golden clouds above him, and he is received up out of their sight.

Years come and go till the little ones have become men and women. The father's beard and the father's hair, so black and heavy at first, have become thin and white. He leans upon his staff, and totters manfully on. Son and daughter press around the mother and sustain her feeble form. An atmosphere of love envelops them all. And so they rise higher and still higher, until, in other than earthly light, they stand glorified upon one of the golden summits. They stand upon the mount of vision, earth below and heaven above them. They gaze down upon the long and weary path they have trodden, and see that their life has been one long process of education and purification. That which was but a path of thorns in the passage is changed to a pavement of gold in the retrospect. Flying over the shining track, they see the Angel of God's Providence; and now they know, what once they could not wholly see, that the darkness which had so often passed over them as they journeyed was but the shadow of his blessed wings. But there comes a sound of chariots and horses; the children press up to bid them adieu, the mountains grow radiant with a descending light; a little voice, never forgotten, breaks through the purpling silence like an arrow of silver; and at the sweet word "come," they are withdrawn into the opening glory.

That, my friends, is my vision. Is it all fancy? Is

it all imagination? Is it all poetry? Have you an idea that fancy, or imagination, or poetry can do justice to the grandeur, beauty, and essential glory of a true life? I have only felt, in painting it, how utterly poor I am in the endeavor to express my conception of the highest life of man and woman, by the use of language. That little creed of Mrs. Browning, uttered impulsively in a flash of inspired conviction, has a world of meaning in it that the slow soul does not perceive. "I do believe in God and love," said the sweet songstress; and so do I. With God and love in human life, it becomes essentially a noble and beautiful thing. To live a life thus informed is a peerless privilege—no matter at what cost of transient pain or unremitting toil. It is a thing above professions and callings and creeds. It is a thing which brings to its nourishment all good, and appropriates to its development of power all evil. It is the greatest and best thing under the whole heaven. Place cannot enhance its honor; wealth cannot add to its value. It is the highest thing. Its course lies through true manhood and womanhood, through true fatherhood and motherhood, through true friendship and relationships, of all legitimate and natural sorts whatsoever. It lies through sorrow and pain and poverty, and all earthly discipline. It lies through unswerving truth to God and man. It lies through patient, self-denying heroism. It lies through all heaven-prescribed and conscientious duty, and it leads as straight to heaven's brightest gate, as the track of a sunbeam to the bosom of a flower.

As I look around me, and see how poor, how frivolous, how weak and drivelling a thing life is, as it is lived by the mass of those who are married, I confess that I am filled with wonder and with pity. Marriage is too much a convention,—its habits and duties are too much conventional. That it is only to be made something better by a change in the general estimate and idea of life, I have said in previous letters. That a man and woman who live to eat, and dress, and make money; whose ends of life are answered in the satisfaction of appetite and ambition, and a thirst for gold and equipage and position, should marry for a higher motive than fancy and convenience, is not to be expected. The structure, therefore, of a true married life, must be laid upon the basis of a true individual life. When men and women have conceived and accepted the idea that all ood in earth and heaven is intended to minister directly and indirectly to individual growth, and that that which we call evil—toil, poverty, sorrow, pain, and temptation to sin—is intended for the development of power and the discipline of passion; when they see that life tends upwards, and is only a preparation for another sphere and a better, and that all that surrounds them is perishable—food and shelter and ministry by the way—then they can have a conception of what true marriage is. The relation is illuminated with its full significance only by this true idea of individual life. The masculine and feminine nature come together for mutual stimulus and mutual feeding. All that is good in each becomes the property of the other, and all that is bad in each is neutralized by the other. Like the acid and the alkali, when brought together, their united life becomes a beaded draught, bland as the juice of nectarines, and fit to sparkle on the lips of an angel.

And now, my friends, farewell! Life is before you,—not earthly life alone, but life—a thread running interminably through the warp of eternity; and while I wish you all manly and womanly joy, and all healthful delight, I do not wish that no pain come on you, no care oppress you, no toil weary you, no sorrow swim in your eyes, no temptations beset you; but I wish that you may bear what God puts upon your shoulders, and bear it well. I wish that it may not be necessary to chasten you overmuch; but you can hardly grow strong without trouble, or sympathetic without sorrow. It was necessary that the only true human life ever lived should be made "perfect through suffering;" and it is strange presumption for you to think that you can be made perfect without it. I wish you many years upon the earth—as many as will minister to your growth and happiness—for life is a sweet as well as a great and wonderful thing. I wish you a family of precious children to fill your homes with music, and enrich your hearts with love. And when, in the evening of life, the golden clouds rest sweetly and invitingly upon the golden mountains, and the light of heaven streams down through the gathering mists of death, I wish you a peaceful and abundant entrance into that world of blessedness, where the great riddle of life, whose meaning I can only hint at, will be unfolded to you in the quick consciousness of a soul redeemed and purified.

THE END.

www.ingramcontent.com/pod-product-compliance
Lightning Source LLC
LaVergne TN
LVHW010256110826
845151LV00004B/1485
* 9 7 8 1 4 2 5 5 2 1 9 7 4 *